"I have a dream that children will one day live where they will not be judged by the color of their skin, but by the content of their character."
— Martin Luther King

I have a dream
words to change the world

- MOTIVATE your pupils to write and appreciate poetry.
- INSPIRE them to share their hopes and dreams for the future.
- BOOST awareness of your school's creative ability.
- WORK alongside the National Curriculum or the high level National Qualification Skills.
- Supports the *Every Child Matters - Make a Positive Contribution* outcome.
- Over £7,000 of great prizes for schools and pupils.

"When I was out there I was never ever alone, there was always a team of people behind me, in mind if not in body."
— Ellen MacArthur

Gloucestershire
Edited by Allison Dowse

Young Writers

First published in Great Britain in 2006 by:
Young Writers
Remus House
Coltsfoot Drive
Peterborough
PE2 9JX
Telephone: 01733 890066
Website: www.youngwriters.co.uk

All Rights Reserved

© *Copyright Contributors 2006*

SB ISBN 1 84602 491 9

Foreword

Imagine a teenager's brain; a fertile yet fragile expanse teeming with ideas, aspirations, questions and emotions. Imagine a classroom full of racing minds, scratching pens writing an endless stream of ideas and thoughts . . .

. . . Imagine your words in print reaching a wider audience. Imagine that maybe, just maybe, your words can make a difference. Strike a chord. Touch a life. Change the world. Imagine no more . . .

'I Have a Dream' is a series of poetry collections written by 11 to 18-year-olds from schools and colleges across the UK and overseas. Pupils were invited to send us their poems using the theme 'I Have a Dream'. Selected entries range from dreams they've experienced to childhood fantasies of stardom and wealth, through inspirational poems of their dreams for a better future and of people who have influenced and inspired their lives.

The series is a snapshot of who and what inspires, influences and enthuses young adults of today. It shows an insight into their hopes, dreams and aspirations of the future and displays how their dreams are an escape from the pressures of today's modern life. Young Writers are proud to present this anthology, which is truly inspired and sure to be an inspiration to all who read it.

Contents

Balcarras School
Alice Bray (11)	1
Rhys Williams (12)	1
Jess Powell (13)	2
Matthew Diesel (12)	3
Beth Coppard (12)	4
Kim Assemat (14)	4
Emily Machin (11)	5
Chloë Mortimer-Stokes (12)	5
Hannah Churchill (12)	6
Azaria Timms (13)	7
Sara Paterson (11)	8
Laurel Townsend (11)	8
Tabitha Robinson-Wall (12)	9
Ben Haines (11)	9
Chris Folland (14)	10
Louis Gill (11)	10
Hannah Douglass (13)	11
Ailsa Hickey (14)	11
Jenny Charlton (11)	12
Kyle Read (11)	13
Bonnie Gibbons (13)	14
Charlotte Annan (11)	14
Eve Dimery (11)	15
Emily Coote (12)	15
James Bagshaw (12)	16
Ben Hodges (12)	16
Jake Flower (12)	17
Jack Green (11)	17
Harry Davis (11)	18
Cavan Costello (12)	18
Warren Cannon (12)	19
Clem Beauchamp (12)	19
Sunicha Chinda (11)	20
Thomas Clarke (11)	20
Thomas Williams (12)	21
Chrissey Worrall (13)	21
Kate Austin (12)	22
Clare Moliver (12)	22

Lois Kingscott (12)	23
Elliot Bishop (11)	23
Steven Veal (11)	24
Victoria Thomas (12)	24
Rebecca Jacombs (11)	25
Becky Peach (13)	25
Laura Stagg (14)	26
Philippa Jordan (12)	27
Abigail Kingscott (12)	28
Sophie Hart (12)	28
Gemma Foulkes (13)	29
Estelle Dyer (12)	29
Gemma Kingsley (11)	30
Emma Lomas (13)	30
Grace Harris (11)	31
Ashleigh Samuels (11)	32
Georgina Dovey (11)	33
Sam Henderson (12)	33
Faye Briggs (13)	34
Eliza Tait-Bailey (12)	35
Vicky Atkins (13)	36
Nicola Stubbs (13)	37
Madddy Maguire (12)	38
Oliver Gibbs (14)	39
Abi Sheridan (11)	40
Freya Toyne (12)	41
James Whistler (12)	42
Mhairi Duck (12)	43
Phoebe Harris (12)	44
Marko Andjelkovic (11)	45
Leah Edwards (13)	46
Megan Sandalls (12)	47
Emma D'Arcy (13)	48
Steph Manifold (14)	49
Clarice Elliott-Berry (12)	50
Jack Thompson (11)	51
Grace Haly (12)	52
Charles Moreton (11)	53
Isabella Abell (12)	54
Annabel Spires (12)	55
Mia Dodds (11)	56
Louise Tottman (11)	57

Emma Malloy (11)   58
Ben Price (11)   59

Barnwood Park School
Becky Franklin (13)   59
Lauren Price (14)   60
Kayleigh Huntley (12)   60
Shakirat Adesanya (14)   61
Sophie Meadows (13)   61
Laura Corrick (12)   62
Charlie Izatt (11)   62
Shelby Hopkins (11)   63
Kirsty-Louise Hardy (11)   63
Helen Overs (12)   64
Chloe Riddick (11)   64
Chloe Tonks (11)   65
Elizabeth Baber (12)   65
Victoria Cooper (12)   66
Leanne Rutledge & Rosie Evans (13)   67
Georgia Ellmore (12)   68
Katie Clutterbuck (12)   68
Carrie Talbot (13)   69
Jess Hollyhead (11)   69
Poppy Thompson (11)   70
Lauren Dickson (11)   70
Hollie Jones (12)   71
Katy Mace (11)   71
Katie Harris (11)   72
Laura Stokes (11)   73
Carlie Baker (12)   74
Amanda Bennett (15)   75
Melanie Clement (12)   76
Katriona Stuart (14)   77
Amy Garbett (12)   78
Philisha Tyne (12)   79
Tammy Hiam (11)   80
Laura Bevan (11)   80
Abbie Phillips (14)   81

Belmont Special Needs School
Jonathan Carr (13) — 82
Alex Gibbons (12) — 82
Kirstie Grainger (14) — 83
Sylvia Aboagye (12) — 83
Michael Tilling (15) — 84

Heywood Community School
George Grindle (13) — 84
Matthew Hawkins (12) — 84
Heidi Beddington (12) — 85
Shannon Roberts (12) — 85
Sophie Coombs (13) — 85
Nikola Michelle Price (14) — 86
Ellie Turner (11) — 86
Claire Herbert (12) — 87
Charlie Roberts (12) — 87
Rebecca Green (15) — 88
Kate Baldwin (12) — 88
Lilia Osborne (12) — 89
Sarah Jelf (12) — 89
Natalie Bonser — 90
Katie Weatherley (12) — 90
Izzie Gazzard (13) — 91
Billy Head (12) — 91
Jenny Salter (13) — 92
Joy Fellows (12) — 92
Robert Elmer (12) — 93
Jordan Taylor (12) — 93
Jordan James (12) — 94
Lydia Holford (13) — 94
Amelia Wheatstone (13) — 95
Samantha Meek (12) — 95

Newent Community School
Jenny Forrester (12) — 95
Erin Taylor (12) — 96
Sydney Foster (13) — 97
Nathaniel Barker (12) — 98
Lydia Buckley (11) — 98

Jack Baker (11)	99
Lewis Pritchard (12)	99
Miriam Vesma (12)	100
Jay Timney (12)	101
Elise Goulding (13)	102
Lorna Baggett (13)	103
Iain Docherty (13)	104
Julia Greenwood (13)	104
Will Jenkins (13)	105
Matthew Eastwood (11)	105
Clare Kerr (13)	106
Carolyn Quinn (12)	106
Anna Charlesworth (13)	107
Ben Norman (12)	107
Emily Suckling (12)	108
Danielle Trevail (12)	109
Matthew Wathen (11)	110
Sam Owen (12)	110
Charlotte Rimmer (12)	111
Jack Davis (11)	111
Sarah Granville (13)	112
Emily Sladen (13)	113
Alex Bayross (11)	114
Elisabeth Fish (11)	114
Louise Morrisson (11)	115
Luke Kavallares (12)	115
Rachel Egan (12)	116
Bethany Murray (12)	117
Alex Rann (12)	118
Sam Goulding (12)	119
Philippa Maile (11)	120
Verity Moulder (12)	121
Sophie Banyard (13)	122
Rachel Dunn (12)	123
Sarah Parsons (12)	124
Felix Bartlett (11)	125
Julia Tweedie (11)	126
Laiken Bennett (12)	127
Olivia Powell (12)	128
Martha Wright (11)	129
Rob Penny (12)	130
Wednesday Batchelor (12)	131

Charlotte Hickling (12) 132
Laura Price (13) 133
Billie Arnold (13) 134
Issi Chamberlayne (13) 135
Sarah Chorlton (12) 136
Jess Cook (13) 137
Josh Edwards (13) 138
Matthew Gaskins (12) 138
Ruth Cracknell (12) 139
Hannah Lammas (12) 140
Luke Wathen (13) 140
Tim Dulson (13) 141
Ellie Baggett (11) 141

Paternoster Special School
Kelly Marie Andrews (13) 142
Aiden Spencer (13) 142
Cody Davey (13) 142

Severn Vale School
Shannon Cook (14) 143

The Poems

I Had A Dream

Martin Luther King preached
As you may recall
He dreamed of a fair world
For black and white and all

He made a very famous speech
That is known everywhere
He said it's what's inside
Not what colour you bare

But now his wife's a widow
And his children have no dad
He was shot in a rally
It was really very sad

So now ask this question
To your family, friends and you
Was Martin King's voice heard?
Did his dream come true?

Alice Bray (11)
Balcarras School

Dreamworld

I have a dreamworld
In my head
Everywhere you can see my inventions
And truckloads upon truckloads of money
There are hover cars
People living on Mars
Vehicles flying through space
A huge human race
It's amazing; it's a mystery
Poverty is history
People live to two hundred years
No one has any fears
This is my dreamworld.

Rhys Williams (12)
Balcarras School

I Have A Dream

I have a dream
That some day
This will not be true
Around the world
There will not be
Fields full of graves

For one night
I had a dream
In a field of graves
And standing to one side
Were a rich man and a knave

And then the knave did speak
Some words I won't forget
He spoke them to me
His eyes full of regret

It is only right
When men do die
Protecting one another
That when the time does come
They are buried together

But they should be buried
In a grave with a name
A family to mourn them
Not alone

And when I did wake
The following morn
I knew what he said
Was true

For in the world
So many men
Are dead without a name
Not known by their families
I think this a shame

That's why it is my dream
To stop this happening
So no men will be buried
In a field full of graves.

Jess Powell (13)
Balcarras School

I Have A Dream

I have a dream

H illy grasslands all around
A perfect land I had found
D ead now though

A land with no woe

D eath and despair are unheard
R eality flies like a bird
E verything bright and colourful
A ll just a . . .
M entality

B ack to reality
U nder life to me
T ime's a disability

I n the land of make-believe
T hat I don't believe in anymore!

W eird places every night
E nroute to platform
N ine and ¾
T ime is irrelvevant

G one now though
O ver stormy seas
N ever to be seen again
E ver!

Matthew Diesel (12)
Balcarras School

I Have A Dream!

I have a dream of children crying
I have a dream of people dying

All these things happen in our country
I want to stop them are you with me?

We need to make the world a better place
So we can stay in the human race

I have a dream of how the world should be
But at the moment we will have to see

Now my dream has come to an end
It has changed my life which I should mend.

Beth Coppard (12)
Balcarras School

I Have A Dream

I am a seed
Small, insignificant
No one knows me
I am tiny

In my dream I am
Big, important
Tall as the sky
Wide as the ocean

I want to be
Strong, impressive
I won't be moved
By the wind

I am but a seed
Hoping, wishing
That when I have grown
I will be known.

Kim Assemat (14)
Balcarras School

I Have A Dream

I have a dream, I have a dream
About McFly that was my dream
I went to their concert and I was singing along
But very soon that was all gone

I have a dream, I have a dream
About McFly that was my dream
Next minute I found myself backstage
When I woke up my mum was shouting with rage.

Emily Machin (11)
Balcarras School

I Have A Dream . . .

I have a dream
I have ambition
I have imagination

I will make a difference
In my dream
I will change the world

I will change the lives of people
In my dream
They will be happy again

I will help
In my dream
Do whatever it takes

I have a dream
I have ambition
I have imagination.

Chloë Mortimer-Stokes (12)
Balcarras School

I Have A Dream

I have a dream
To go where every other child has been
The local Mr Chippy
It's only round the corner too, I've seen

I have a dream
And with Daddy, it's just about to come true
I'm his little buttercup
Whenever I smile sweetly he says, 'Anything for you!'

I have a dream
Because Mummy, she thinks we are far too posh
When she saw the bubbling chip fat
And the grease oozing out, all she could say was, 'Oh my golly gosh!'

I had a dream
I knew she'd come around when she'd had a bite
Of those tasty fish and chips
And now we visit every single fortnight!

I have a *new* dream
I've just discovered they sell what's known as Coke
My friends they really love it
But Mummy says that it's only for the common folk!

'Daddy . . . !'

Hannah Churchill (12)
Balcarras School

Daddy Was A Black Man . . .

Daddy was a black man
The white men called him, 'Negro'
Mummy liked the girl next door
The kids all called her 'queer'
My sister has dyslexia
My friends all call her 'stupid'
My uncle liked to wear a dress
They all called him 'sissy'
My brother is an octopus
Now things are getting silly . . .

My best friend is an albino
My classmates call her 'freak'
My cousin is just overweight
Strangers call him 'piggy'
Me? I am normal
Ordinary that's me
But think about it next time you call these people names
Cos they're my family
And if there was a world where we were equal
Then this world would be it
But no one realises yet
Think about it.

Azaria Timms (13)
Balcarras School

I Have A Dream

I did have a dream
A breathtaking dream it was
For me anyway

I dreamed of dolphins
So that I could swim with them
In the wild oceans

I dreamt about sport
About tennis and hockey
I could play better

I dreamt about flight
I could fly to New Zealand
And the Bahamas

I wish I could keep
My friends for evermore and
Keep in touch with them

I did have some dreams
Some breathtaking dreams they were
For me anyway.

Sara Paterson (11)
Balcarras School

I Have A Dream

I have a dream
Where black and white
Have to unite
Their feelings are non-racist
And their friendships are everlasting
Black and white forever together
Even at the park and slide
Black and white will harvest together
Not afraid by their colour or brother or mother.

Laurel Townsend (11)
Balcarras School

I Have A Dream

I have a dream
I had a dream
Pigs were flying
Sheep were multiplying

I like a dream
I liked a dream
I was with my mates
Then I made a big mistake

I love a dream
I loved a dream
I was a model
From then on life was a doddle

I hate a dream
I hated a dream
I was falling
No one answered. I kept on calling!

I have a dream
I had a dream
Alarm bells ringing, Mum with a teacup
Oh my gosh! It's time to get up!

Tabitha Robinson-Wall (12)
Balcarras School

I Have A Dream

Stop cruelty to animals
Do not abandon them
Care for them
Train them properly
Give shelter to them
Put food and water out for them
Give donations to the RSPCA
Don't be a poacher.

Ben Haines (11)
Balcarras School

I Had A Dream

The stifling heat waved at the sky
Performing a dance for the fiery desert
The horned skull of a long dead beast jutted out of the sand
It grinned at me as I passed, mocking me

A gust of sandy wind, brushed past me
Racing and howling with rage
Tumbleweed fled past me in fear of the oncoming storm
They sped off, as if in the Grand National

A great fiery monster lifted its terrifying head
It roared a gust of ash and fire
I sprinted away
But flames were dancing all around

The beast roared with laughter
As the acrid smoke rose high
Flickering images flittered across my sight
The skull; the flames . . .

'And that was my dream Mum.'
I finished up my toast and went to school.

Chris Folland (14)
Balcarras School

Dream

I know a thing called a dream
Being the star of the team
It's a wonderful feeling
And very appealing
But sometimes boring so it seems

So what is your big dream?
So what is your big scheme?
Scoring the goal
Or drilling a hole
But after all it is just a dream.

Louis Gill (11)
Balcarras School

Nightmare

I'm running, never stopping, for the terror that surrounds me
Has no sympathy, no guilt, no limit and no boundary
It's strangling me, mangling me, heart tearing wildly
And leading me somewhere so horrific and yet imaginary

My feet tremble uncontrollably, as they walk the dreaded stairs
My eyes weep silently, avoiding ghostly glares
For I'm not alone and soon I'll find the man slumped in his chair
He'll beckon me and I'll go to him, mesmerised and unawares

He brandishes the dagger, bloodstains glinting in the light
But just as the blade penetrates . . . I wake to a welcoming sight
My bedroom, it was just a dream, however there's no end to this fright;
Because I know I will meet the man again . . . tomorrow night.

Hannah Douglass (13)
Balcarras School

Dreaming Time

I drifted up the stairs
Gone are the worldly cares
I've been told my night rhyme
And now it's dreaming time

Swashbuckle the pirate I may visit tonight
Sail until dawn breaks the first light
Or a crown to be a princess
With everything in the world no less

I get nightmares of a snake
How I long to be awake
I see its huge teeth
Which I don't want to be underneath

That only happens on bad days
I usually wake up almost always
The alarm rings I know it is time
To finish those wild dreams of mine.

Ailsa Hickey (14)
Balcarras School

I Have A Dream

I have a dream
It's scary
About a person being murdered
Called Mary

Her scary scream slips
Back into the darkness
Next all you hear is a
Lark that passes

I wake up all of a sudden
It's late, the clock is ticking
Everything is still
Then I realise
Things are as they should be

Someone else's dream
However
Could be as light as
A feather

No deadly and dark torturing
Screams
Instead you see God's hand
In bright light beams

Dreams are not as they seem
To be
They are in our heads
You see.

Jenny Charlton (11)
Balcarras School

I Had A Dream

I had a dream
On a ship
On the sea
With the wind
Whistling through my hair

I had my dream
On the ship
On the sea
With but one
Bright and little flare

I had my dream
On the ship
On the sea
My only flare
Was unseen

I had my dream
On the ship
On the sea
And the water leaked in
Beneath my feet

I had my dream
On the ship
On the sea
As my ship
Plunged down into the sea.

Kyle Read (11)
Balcarras School

Dreams

Dreams are where most children go
A land draped in none but snow
A place of joy and happiness
A bed of clouds for one to rest
A reflection of the day's events
No home to the smallest bit of sense

But sometimes to follow a dreary day
A dream can go and run astray
To a different place, far from joy
A world of darkness and evil ploys
A child would hate to near this zone
Close by, you can hear them moan

So keep your distance in this land
Be well behaved, obedient and
You can be sure, your dreams will stay
Closer to the light of day.

Bonnie Gibbons (13)
Balcarras School

I Have A Dream

The ground is parched, the river dies
The poor people have no supplies
The cold night air is cut with cries

With stuck out bones like blunted knives
And bellies swollen twice the size
The people cling to fading lives

I see their pain in bulging eyes
And faces gaunt and thick with flies
I cannot watch as someone dies

My dream is easy to accomplish
Quite simply to stop all of this
That's yours and mine's forever wish.

Charlotte Annan (11)
Balcarras School

I Have A Dream

I have a dream
A world where the sky is never grey
Where suffering is lessened day by day
Where nobody cares about whether you're young or you're old
Or even whether you're shy or you're bold
Where poverty really is history
Where everybody is treated just the same
Black people and white people, the hurt and the lame
Where people don't just dump trash and litter
And the taste of pain is not so bitter
Where debt and terrorism does not exist
But I know that too long in writing is this list
Where it doesn't matter about your odour or your race
I have a dream where the world is a better place.

Eve Dimery (11)
Balcarras School

I Have A Dream

I have a dream that all is loved
All feelings were deep
And the love would keep

I have a nightmare where all was heartbroken
And nothing of love was spoken
Everyone was confused of their feelings
Like they were all muddled up to the ceilings

I have a dream where true love is not forgotten
But stays in your heart
And always has a part

But not all dreams come true
So let's start over
With someone new.

Emily Coote (12)
Balcarras School

I Have A Dream

Once I dreamt a dream, I dreamt a dream
That I was flying so high
Among the silky, deep blue sky

All a sudden my house, I could see
With the back door and the chimney

As I was there, flying so high
The clouds were dancing in the sky

The sun was shining, shining so bright
I saw the brilliant powerful light

Once I dreamt, I dreamt a dream
That I was flying so high
Among the silky, deep blue sky

My dream soon ended
I stood there suspended
My dream was over
I no longer flew so high above the sky.

James Bagshaw (12)
Balcarras School

I Have A Dream

I have a dream
Where the world is clean
Helping to make poverty
Part of history
I have a dream
Where every being
Is always met
With great respect
I have a dream
Where no one's keen
To hurt another
Whose skin is a different colour
I have a dream!

Ben Hodges (12)
Balcarras School

I Had A Dream

Where am I? What am I doing? What has happened?
I wonder around tentatively, staring into the foggy darkness that surrounds me
Gravestones cover the floor, of both the rich and poor
My eyes scan the scene, trees crowd me in darkness
I am enclosed yet I am exposed
What was that? I see a movement, a flicker, a glimmer
I'm scared stiff. I can't move. My mind is telling me to run but my legs won't obey
I hear a *bang!* I turn on the spot. Was that the shot of a gun?
My heart is pounding, my world spinning, my legs obey and I start to run
I tear into the trees, towards the darkness, I am in a forest
No light meets my eye, but I carry on anyway
Then my heart sinks, my body too, I'm frozen with fear, what can I do?
I start falling, gathering speed, I have no life left in me
Further and further down I fall then . . .
Darkness!

Jake Flower (12)
Balcarras School

I Have A Dream . . .

That all people in this world
Will be loving and will be kind
And all sadness in this world
Shall be left behind

That all children on this Earth
Are deeply loved and cared for
That they all enjoy a happy life
With families they adore

That there is no hatred
Let all war cease
And that all race and religions
Shall be at peace
That is my dream.

Jack Green (11)
Balcarras School

I Have A Dream

I had a dream that there would be no more fighting and no
more arguments
I had a dream that all wars would stop and that all countries
would make up for all the silly things that they have done in the past
I had a dream where nobody was mean and horrible
I had a dream that no one would die
I had a dream that animals and humans would stop being silly
and doing things that they would regret
and just enjoy life as it does not last for long
I had a dream that everyone was always happy and never sad
I had a dream that soon came true.

Harry Davis (11)
Balcarras School

I Have A Dream

I have a dream
To end poverty
That children in Africa run around
Not worried about them dying of AIDS
Or about their parents dying and
Leaving them as orphans
With nobody to look after them or love them

I have a dream
That children everywhere
On the streets
Get put into a home
With a loving caring family
That looks after them so they have no more worries

That's my dream, what's yours?

Cavan Costello (12)
Balcarras School

Dream

I have a dream
I have lots of ice cream
And chocolate doughnuts
In my little hut
At the end of the garden

I have a dream
That it seems
That every day I have more chocolate
Filling my little hut
At the end of my garden

I have a dream
I've eaten lots of ice cream
And now it's turning into a nightmare
Not that I care
I just eat and eat

I have a nightmare
That I'm really fat in there
I hope this will stop
Or I think I will pop
I want to get out of this nightmare.

Warren Cannon (12)
Balcarras School

I Have A Dream

I have a dream
That there is no pollution
Cars run on water
And let out air

I have a dream
That all races of people can be friends
They can live happily
Together.

Clem Beauchamp (12)
Balcarras School

I Have A Dream

I have a dream that one day all my family
Will have their own houses
And I will bring them to England to live forever
And we will be very happy together

I have a dream that I will be a doctor
Helping people get better
Save their lives and it will be very sad
When they die - and that is my dream . . .

Sunicha Chinda (11)
Balcarras School

I Have A Dream!

I have a dream
That the world was covered in cream
I have a dream
That people had laser beams
I have a dream
That time was flying by
I have a dream
Where people could fly
I have a dream
Where people die
I have a dream
That animals ate pie
I have a dream
That things were black and white
I have a dream
Where everything was bright
I have a dream
Which no one could fight
So that's my dream
Day and night!

Thomas Clarke (11)
Balcarras School

My Dream

My dream would be for everything to reach perfection
But what is the power of a dream if it does not yet exist?
What is a dream anyway?
A collection of random images
Or a crazy thought that is impossible to gain

What we want, we have to achieve
But if we keep dreaming up ideas that just can't happen
Then how do we have the time to achieve what can happen?

We don't
So my dream would be for there to be no dreams
To give us time to get to our target
To reach *perfection*.

Thomas Williams (12)
Balcarras School

I Have A Dream

I have a dream
Of brooks and fountains
To sit by up in the mountains

I have a dream
Of people and places
A mix of ages and races

I have a dream
Of princesses and knights
Starting a fight

I have a dream
Of hostages and heroes
Against evil Nero

I have a dream
Of mice and men
Kept in a child's den.

Chrissey Worrall (13)
Balcarras School

I Have A Dream

I have a dream
That one day
Everyone will be happy
Glad they're living on this Earth
Without pain and misery

I have a dream
That one day
There will be no poverty
All will have enough to drink and eat
And a shelter to sleep and live

I have a dream
That one day
All war will be done for
Countries will live in peace and comfort
Guns will be banned for evermore

I have a dream
That one day
This dream will be a reality.

Kate Austin (12)
Balcarras School

I Have A Dream

Everyone can achieve their dream
If you just believe
Whatever you want to do
You can
If you just believe
If you want to be a doctor
If you want to do
All you have to say is
I will do
What I want to.

Clare Moliver (12)
Balcarras School

I Had A Dream

I'll skate on ice for Britain today
And hopefully win gold
Gliding softly on my skates
Through the icy cold!

I'll shoot a ball for Britain today
Through the great big hoop!
Playing netball, concentrating
Winning gold with my group!

I'll ride a horse for Britain today
I'll jump five foot four!
And canter round the jumping course
And score the highest score!

I'll wake up slowly, yawning today
And get myself all clean!
I'll think about all the sports I played!
And realise I had a dream!

Lois Kingscott (12)
Balcarras School

I Have A Dream

I have a dream of no war
There will be no fighting
No weapons
Just peace

I have a dream of no criminals
There will be no murder
Just peace

I know this will never happen
Of that I'm totally sure
But I can always keep trying
Hoping that I can make a difference

Will there ever be peace?

Elliot Bishop (11)
Balcarras School

I Have A Dream

I have a dream where the world is a good place
Pollution, death and suffering are nowhere to be seen on its face
Where everything is free
Where everyone lives in perfect peace and harmony
Then I opened my eyes
And noticed that freedom is not free
The world is burning
And still no one would be concerned if it stopped turning.

Steven Veal (11)
Balcarras School

I Have A Dream

(Bullies are losers)

I have a dream that one day
All the bullies would *go away*
It's my life so don't live it
Just cos you're bigger than me

There's more of you than there are of me
Does it make you feel better about yourself
When you make me feel less than you?

You're so insecure
My parents say you're jealous
But it doesn't really feel that way
It seems you find it fun
To pick on me

If I cry
I'm a 'cry baby'

If I tell
I'm a 'dobber'

If I stay put
I'm a 'victim'

If I stand up to you
I will be free . . .

Victoria Thomas (12)
Balcarras School

I Have A Dream

I have a dream that my children will grow up in a world they know
they are safe in
I have a dream that all of us will live in peace
I have a dream that everyone can be what they want to be whatever
shape or size
I have a dream where we are all equal and everyone has the room
to live and the right to live
I have a dream that no one will be rejected by people who think they
are better
When really they are the same.

Rebecca Jacombs (11)
Balcarras School

Dream Or Reality?

I have a dream each night
That Mummy and Daddy are having a fight
Mummy's old vase smashes
And I watch as my life around crashes
All around me

I have a dream in my bed
That I walk in and Ma is bleeding from the head
Beside her is an empty bottle of whiskey
The room starts to swirl and blur around me
I call for help but I know she's gone

I have a dream whilst I'm asleep
That the hospital machinery starts to beep
The doctors and nurses all rush in
And bellow for the next of kin
I'm just pushed aside

I have a dream when the stars come out
That outside I hear a loud shout
My dad's being attacked by a load of white yobs
The blood on the pavement goes into blobs
All because he's 'black'.

Becky Peach (13)
Balcarras School

I Have A Dream

I wander through the streets
I wander down a lane
As I wander, I wonder

I wonder about lots of things
The mountains, the hills, the earth
I wonder about the future, my future

What will become of me?
Will I be successful?
Will I not?

I wonder all these things as I wander
As I walk I wonder even more
Time passes and I'm still thinking

Still wondering

I think of my ambitions
My hopes
My goals

As I wander
I pass people
Lots of people

Each with their own ambition
Their own hopes
Their own goals

All in their own world
With their own thoughts
With their own dreams

They have dreams
Lots of dreams
Millions of dreams

My dream is one of them
One of the millions of dreams in the world
Just one

I have a dream
This is what I think about
Through the streets
And down a lane
This is what I wonder as I wander.

Laura Stagg (14)
Balcarras School

I Have A Dream

The lights flash
My vision blurring
A thunder crash
My voice slurring

A mixed up world
Where nothing's right
The straight lines curled
No day just night

The sky bright blue
A land of cheer
One change, it's new
A world of fear

I scream, I run
My feet stay still
No longer fun
My laughter nil

Then I'm awake
No need to scream
No need to shake
Just a dream.

Philippa Jordan (12)
Balcarras School

I Have A Dream

I have a dream
For the world not one

I have a dream
For those whose life has just begun

I have a dream
Of a world without hate

I have a dream
Set on a date

I have a dream
To last all your life

I have a dream
Of a world without a knife

I have a dream
To all live in peace.

Abigail Kingscott (12)
Balcarras School

I Have A Dream

I dreamed that I was me
And not the girl I want to be
I dreamed I was different
I did what everyone doesn't
I dreamed that I was smart
I didn't have a cold heart
I dreamed I that I was clever
And that was like never

I dreamed my greatest fear
All of it was beginning to appear
I was seeing my true self.

Sophie Hart (12)
Balcarras School

I Have A Dream

I have a dream . . . but all I do is wish
Find a toad and give it a kiss
I could make a palace or dress up in a gown
Pretend I'm a princess, wearing a royal crown

I would attend fancy balls
Even shop in expensive malls!
I would own my very own glass slippers
Have my own butlers who look like penguins in flippers

Oh how fun would life be?
Sitting there with a cup of earl grey tea!
Receiving lots of flowers
I'd be lucky to be the one with the powers

I have a dream . . . but all I can do is wish
Find a toad and give it a kiss.

Gemma Foulkes (13)
Balcarras School

I Have A Dream!

I have a dream
A dream of fear and fright
It makes my tummy feel very tight

I have a dream
A dream of happiness and laughter
Where in the world there is no disaster

I have a dream
A dream of freedom and respect
Of safety when all nationalities collect

I have a dream
A dream of no more sadness and starvation
Which has happened to many in a nation

I have a dream
Where all my dreams come true.

Estelle Dyer (12)
Balcarras School

I Have A Dream

I wish that people who are shallow
Shall drown in their sorrows
And one day we might all as well be blind

But that is a doubt
The probability is poor
As looks are only important to low lifes
And no one else

Some people say we are born with our attitude
They are wrong
We make our attitudes

Why does it matter if we are
Fat or thin, curved or straight, tall or small, black or white?
The answer is, it doesn't!

Gemma Kingsley (11)
Balcarras School

I Have A Dream

I have a dream
That one day
The world was treated fairly
Famine was fought
Drought was done
No one was homeless
No one was sick
Food was plentiful
Crime was no more

I have a dream
That one day
People were treated fairly
I dreamt that poverty was in the past
The world was a better place
But after all
It was just a dream.

Emma Lomas (13)
Balcarras School

I Have A Dream

Wars will never be over
I want them to be
Poverty goes on
Make it stop
Natural disasters take lives
We can't stop them

People who suffer
In faraway lands
On our lands too
Those people have dreams
Dreams for a better life
They have dreams

Wars go on
Innocent die
They got what they wanted
Leave us alone
It's their dreams
That's their dreams

Disasters eat lives
Like a lion on prey
Tsunamis and earthquakes
Break families apart
Take their dreams
No dreams left

I have a dream
Many of them
Everybody has a dream
Some people have them stolen
By their lives
I have a dream . . . do it.

Grace Harris (11)
Balcarras School

I Have A Dream

I have a dream
That everything is free
I have a dream
That there are no schools
I have a dream
Where all the countries are treated the same
I have a dream
Where you would have more than one life
I have a dream
Where people who are 13 or over can learn to drive
I have a dream
That I will become a football player
I have a dream
Where all people who live on the streets get a house to live in
I have a dream
Where no one would lie
I have a dream
That money starts falling down from the sky
I have a dream
Where I can speak all the languages in the world
I have a dream
Where all trees are blue
I have a dream
Where the sky is green
I have a dream
Where the clouds are pink
I have a dream.

Ashleigh Samuels (11)
Balcarras School

I Have A Dream

I had a dream
Where my dream came true
A happy dream
A funny dream
A confusing dream
I had a dream

I had a dream
Where my dream was pretend
A scary dream
A nightmare
A terrifying dream
I had a dream

I had a dream
Where my dream was my life, my future
It was a fantastic dream
A great dream
A perfect dream
I had a dream

I *have* a dream
And my dream is a wish
My wishes are to . . .
Win the lottery
Get a good job
And make all my other wishes come true!
That is my dream!

Georgina Dovey (11)
Balcarras School

I Have A Dream

You, me, everyone around us have different dreams at night
Some people hate peace and just want to have a fight
But always most people do prefer no war, just happiness
And that is why I have written this nagging verse.

Sam Henderson (12)
Balcarras School

I Have A Dream . . .

My family gone
Gone to God knows where
I just woke up
And they weren't there

Three years old
A baby girl
Just sitting cold
With mother's pearl

Where do I go? What do I do?
How do I survive
Without you?

All alone on my bedroom floor
Wondering, wondering
Who is next through that door

Who could do this
How cruel and mean?
Me, watching . . . waiting . . . wishing
Wishing this was a dream.

Faye Briggs (13)
Balcarras School

I Have A Dream

Dreams can be make-believe
Dreams can be true
Dreams can be scary
With ghosts that say, 'Boo!'

Dreams can be great
Dreams can be fun
Dreams can be happy
Like winning a run

Are you asleep or are you awake?
Is your dream true life
Or just a story (a fake)?
Does your dream come straight from your head
Or is your dream in your life out of your bed?

My dream is part of life not part of nights
I believe everyone has equal rights
But I still have dreams when I sleep in bed
With all of the people that live in my head

They tell me stories
Some scary, some cute
But there's one source
Like a tree with a root
This makes my dream be in life or in bed
It's all what I think about
It's all in my head.

Eliza Tait-Bailey (12)
Balcarras School

I Had A Dream

I had a dream that everything was opposite, back to front
Black was white and white was black
Similarities were completely different
Books started with 'The End' and ended at the beginning

I had a dream that nothing was new and the world was only a copy
Free will wasn't frowned upon, but would have been if it had existed
People had the bodies of humans but the instincts of sheep; just follow
the person
in front
Why do something original when you can do something that someone
else has
done before?

I had a dream that people had their own choice of future
Your whole life doesn't have to depend on if you were born in a
mansion or on the streets
People saw you for who you were, not how big your income was

After all, who cares how much money you have?
And what does it matter how big your house is?

Then I woke up and realised
People do judge you on the colour
Of your skin, your job and how
Much money you have.

Vicky Atkins (13)
Balcarras School

I Have A Dream

I have a dream . . .

When I stand alone I watch them play
I vanish in a corner, the one safe place to stay . . .

I never retaliate or say anything back
But strength and courage is the one thing I lack

What can I do but stand there and cry
I watch people of authority just pass me by

My words have been quiet, but my weeping never silent
That began to happen when things turned violent

Sticks and stones will break my bones
But bruises never heal when I'm alone

My mother often asks why I am so down
So I smile at her sweetly to hide my growing frown

Each tear that falls heavy down my cheek
Just adds to the sorrow and sadness of my week

I'm just another girl, or so it may seem
But if you look at me closely you'll see, 'I have a dream . . .'

A dream to stop the tears, a dream to stop the pain
A dream to be accepted and learn to live again.

Nicola Stubbs (13)
Balcarras School

I Have A Dream

I have a dream
That we see the real picture
Not the frame around it
Whether black or white
Green or blue
It's the beauty of the picture that truly counts
No matter who we are

I have a dream
That the colour of our skin proves nothing
I have a dream
The epic sunshine
Only shines where the true
Earth belongs

I have a dream
We're all one
Accepting for who we are
I have a dream
We forget the past
And run fast
Because we are all equal
We should wake up and
Live the dream
Forever and ever.

Madddy Maguire (12)
Balcarras School

I Have A Dream

I have a dream
A fantastic dream
I'm bowling for England
In the England cricket team
Running at the batter
The wind in my eyes
I come up to the crease
And let the ball fly
It whistles down the wicket
Swerving as it goes
It's going 90 mph
Pitching at the batsman's toes
It takes the off-stump out the ground
Missing the batter's bat
People are jumping up and down
I hear cries of, 'Howzat!'
'We've won, we've won,' my teammates shout
'Nice bowl,' my coaches say
I've won the Ashes for my team
I hope it comes true some day.

Oliver Gibbs (14)
Balcarras School

I Have Dreams

I have a dream
A fantasy
To help me through
Reality

I have a dream
That no one knows
An abandoned house
Where no one goes

I have a dream
Where no one is sad
It helps me cope
With good and bad

I have a dream
To mix all races
It's inside that counts
Not the colour of faces

I have a dream
All hunger gone
Everyone's full
Under the shining sun

I have a dream
People over the globe
Are treated equal
No rags no robes

I have a dream
To end all wars
Fighting like this
Should be against the law

My dreams all have a meaning
If you look close you will see
The answer to all problems
To the locks we've found the key.

Abi Sheridan (11)
Balcarras School

I Have A Dream

I've dreamt of the stage
From a very young age
There's a buzz in my chest
As the crowd comes to rest
I see their faces beam at me
Then it comes over me
The power to act like magic it comes!
My lines they flow
Rolling straight off my tongue
My eyes alight with passion
As though it were an everyday fashion

My soul is placed
Without any trace
As an actress through and through
To speak the wonders
Of theatrical dance!
The audience becomes entranced
By my acting at their very first glance

I put on my costume
Whoosh! I'm off
I'm whoever I'm dressed to be!
The important thing
I'm sure you'll agree
Is that when I'm performing
There's not a trace of me
I've fled!
I'm dead!
Hung up!
Disappeared for good
Until the curtain closes.

Freya Toyne (12)
Balcarras School

I Have A Dream

I have a dream, a dream to end poverty
No more people living in boxes
Food for everyone, rich and poor
Lack of clean water reduced to a scarcity

I have a dream, a dream for world peace
Wars to be over, the arguments stopped
For land to be shared, not greedily taken
Tolerance and acceptance to greatly increase

I have a dream, a dream to end racism
The colour of your skin should not matter at all
A world without prejudice, equality all around
Religion and nationality not leading to terrorism

I have lots of dreams that I wish would all come true
I wish that everyone was equal, not rich or poor
That what you looked like made no difference
I wish the world was never old, and everything stayed new.

James Whistler (12)
Balcarras School

I Have A Dream

I have a dream
That if everyone was an apple
We could get rid of all the rotten ones
Then the world would be an orchard of fresh apples

I have a dream
That if everyone was a blade of grass
We could get rid of all the brown ones
Then the world would be a field of green grass

I have a dream
That if everyone was a shell
We could get rid of all the cracked ones
Then the world would be a beach of perfect shells

I have a dream
Of a perfect world . . .

Mhairi Duck (12)
Balcarras School

My Dream . . .

That look reminds me of a summer's night
The air full of sorrow
Not happiness and delight
The sky red and purple
The screams ruin the beautiful sight
Alone, in a world full of hate

That look reminds me of a winter's morn
Thousands of people
Looking forlorn
The sky blue and grey
Their lives twisted and torn
Alone in a world full of hate

That look reminds me of a world that could be
A world where all happiness is let out free
One which is better for you and for me
That would be *my* dream.

Phoebe Harris (12)
Balcarras School

I Have A Dream

I have a dream
To be a footballer
Where I score lots of goals
And win every match

I have a dream
For world peace
When people help each other
And there are no more wars

I have a dream
To make poverty history
So no one goes hungry
And suffering stops

I have a dream
For a cure for every illness
So people would not die
And can live a longer life.

Marko Andjelkovic (11)
Balcarras School

I Have A Dream

The sun was shining, the grass was green
It was actually happening - the thing I always dream
I was walking out on to the pitch, I couldn't believe it
My face was full of delight, you should have seen it
Holding Thierry Henry's hand and leading him out
Something I always wanted to do and dreamt about

The sun was shining, I was chilling by the pool
In Mauritius where the breeze is refreshing and cool
Reading my book, licking a lolly
Everyone's mood was cheerful and jolly
Happy as can be. All in good spirit
This was a place I had always dreamt I would visit

The sun was shining and glaring onto my glasses
Lead there on the beach as a group of people passes
Getting a tan in my new bikini
On a beach in Cali you should have seen me
A smile on my face as wide as can be
I always dreamt of being there as you could probably see.

Leah Edwards (13)
Balcarras School

I Have A Dream

My dream
It didn't seem true at first
At first it wasn't
But now it is
My dream is to travel
To travel in time
To see what it was like then
When you are where you are, you don't know
What it was like back then
To travel over good times
And bad times too
To see wars
And times where people didn't know the things we know now
I met people that said, 'Hello,' but they were
Not like people back at home
I don't really like it here
It's strange and weird and not like home
I've fulfilled my dream though
I like it at home
And I always will
I'm not going any further.

Megan Sandalls (12)
Balcarras School

Without Dreams

Images, ideas, aspirations, freedom, hope
Dreams are our motivation
Our stop and go
Our inspiration
Our thoughts, our feelings
Our hopes and fears
They are the world inside our heads
As we dream, so we escape
We can be who we want to be
We can do what we want to do
We can see what we want to see
No boundaries
No restrictions
No limits
Dreams set us free

But life without dreams
Would be no life at all
Nothing to get up for when the early sunlight screams through the window
No kick from the non-existent thoughts of what the day will bring
Dreams help us shine, dreams help us sing
Without dreams there would be no man on the moon
No surfing the net
No surfing on sea
Dreams set us free
Dreams make you you
And me me.

Emma D'Arcy (13)
Balcarras School

I Have A Dream . . .

I wake at night, it's dark, no light
I'm holding something gold and bright
My Olympic medal, heavy and gleaming
Is it true or am I dreaming?
It's 2012, the London games
I trained to win, I wanted the fame
My horse was ready, fit and strong
His jump was high, his stride was long

The riding was against the clock
Time to gallop not to trot
Moving fast just like a train
With flailing hooves and a flowing mane
The rustic poles, the ditch and water
My mother watching her youngest daughter
Flying past the spiky gorse
That formed the jumps and lined the course
Lining up for a mighty leap
Up a bank so very steep
Making sure I do not fall
Knowing that the winner takes all

The medal firmly in my grasp
Or do I fall at the very last?

Does my story have a tragic theme
Or do I win as in my dream?

Steph Manifold (14)
Balcarras School

I Have A Dream

One day there'll be no poverty, no starving, no war!
This day will come at the end of time
People roam the Earth no more
One day there'll be no murder, no fighting, no theft!
This day will come at the end of time
When nobody is left
But I have a dream, unlikely it may be
Where everyone is living oh so peacefully!

One day there'll be no flooding, no sadness, no drought
This day will come at the end of time
When nobody's about
One day there'll be no pollution, no famine, no disease!
This day will come at the end of time
Nothing there just peace!
But I have a dream, unlikely it may be, where everyone is living, oh so
happily
Together!

Clarice Elliott-Berry (12)
Balcarras School

The Dream

Why is the world always so unhappy? It's unbelievable
I've seen the misery everyone holds
The anger and the rage that's piercing our souls
A swarm of sullen faces, walking through the streets
Arguing and fighting with everybody they meet
How can we change this? How can we learn?
Am I the only person in the world who's concerned?

I dream about this every day, the thought doesn't leave my head
Why can't we change the world and make things right like when I'm dreaming in bed?
Let's enjoy our lives, live them fully. Live it like a king
Just smile and laugh and join the joy and happiness you will bring

I dream in magic, I dream in peace
A dream of happiness that I can release
The dream has changed me and things must be different
The anger, the hatred and also the rage
Stop these things of this day of age
I know I can help the world to smile
The world will shine and stop being vile.

Jack Thompson (11)
Balcarras School

I Have A Dream

I wish for world peace
That all violence would cease
Everyone would be friends
Until the world ends

I wish it were summer all year round
No wind, no rain just peace all around
The birds would sing
Like they do in spring

I wish people would share
They would share and they'd care
No one mean
All just keen

I wish the world were clean
And a very pretty scene
Not a drop of litter
The bins would glitter

I wish the world were honest
Not lie and be dishonest
We could trust the people we meet
Be friends and not cheat

My dreams may not come true
But I will help myself get through
I have fun in my life
And ignore all the fights

I wish for world peace
That all violence would cease
Everyone would be friends
Until the world ends.

Grace Haly (12)
Balcarras School

I Have A Dream

I have six dreams
The first one is this
All my dreams come true with bliss

My second dream
Is to be
Captain of a team
Of England rugby

My third dream
Is to be
The richest man
Earth has even seen

My fourth dream
Destroys poverty
Gives everyone a house
In 2014

My fifth dream
Blanks out cruelty
From the biggest land animals
To the smallest in the sea

My sixth dream
Is to win the Guinness Premiership
For Gloucester rugby team
With lots of sponsorship.

Charles Moreton (11)
Balcarras School

I Have A Dream

I wish we could find
Find, find, find
All the happiness in the world

I wish we could share
Share, share, share
All our hopes and dreams

I wish we could live
Live, live, live
In peace and harmony

I wish we could give
Give, give, give
Our most prized possessions

I wish we could be free
Free, free, free
As a soaring bird . . .

. . . I wish this was our world!

Isabella Abell (12)
Balcarras School

I Have A Dream

I have a dream
Of no fighting
I have a dream
Of no war
I want to watch the TV
And hear of peace not war

I want people to be kind to each other
For nobody to fight
I wish the bad in the world would go
And everyone is happy and at peace

I have a dream
That no one goes hungry
Or dies of disease
I want no one to be poor
And always have fresh water
This is my dream.

Annabel Spires (12)
Balcarras School

I Have A Dream

I had a dream
To be a star
Go on stage
Sing, dance, act

I would be famous
Signing autographs
People screaming for me
Wow! I'd be rich!

Hang on
I am only a kid
How am I going to be a star?

I could be a director, telling celebrities where to stand
Making films
I could win awards

MTV best director, oh thank you
Thank you

Then again
I might just get a job
Be a teacher. Yeah!
That's my dream!

Mia Dodds (11)
Balcarras School

I Have A Dream

I have a dream
That the world is full of laughter
I have a dream
Everyone lives happily ever after
I have a dream
Of fluffy white kittens
I have a dream
Of rabbits in mittens
I have a dream
Of sweeties galore
I have a dream
That no one is poor
I have a dream
Of floating up high
I have a dream
Of a clear blue sky
I have a dream
That my wishes come true
So I can share them with people just like you!

Louise Tottman (11)
Balcarras School

I Have A Dream . . .

I would like to do well at school
But I would not like to rule the school
I will do well in exams
And I will probably take commands

I am sure I would like to help people with grief
So they can feel better
And I can feel better for helping them you see
So we can all live with love and company

I would like to become a teacher
Like my mum and her mum and dad
So children can learn
And I don't feel bad

I swim at the moment
I love it so much
I would like to become better
And swim so much
I would like to swim in the Olympics
And swim for my country
Also win medals for me and my family

Everyone has dreams and that might come true
Just believe in yourself
And I am sure you will be great
Whether it's for your country
Other people, your family or just you!

Just believe in yourself
And appreciate other people
And your dreams can come true!

Emma Malloy (11)
Balcarras School

I Have A Dream

I have a dream
Of school not being there
Of teachers eaten by a bear
Of kids doing what they like
Running riot with a pike
Breaking windows with a rock

I have a dream
Where everything is fine
Or go on a shoplifting spree
Steal what we want
Or whatever is out front

I have a dream
Of a giant skate park
Maybe made of wood
If I could
It'll be for BMXs

I have a dream
In fact I have a lot of dreams
And these are just a few!

Ben Price (11)
Balcarras School

Peace?

No guns, no fire, no cold blooded murder
No children screaming, no families grieving

No fires spreading with red-hot anger
No soldiers shouting, riots starting

No bombs exploding, no hostages kept
Wishing, wishing for the freedom

The freedom of peace.

Becky Franklin (13)
Barnwood Park School

My Dreams

My dreams are raging fires
Burning my heart with timeless desires
Kindled by life is my ambition
To have a world of peace is my mission

I will not be put of by those who can't see
Just what my dreams mean to me
Arrogant, a callous bully
Those are things I don't aspire to be

My life, I love, it suits me
An inspiring path to what I want to be
But to show the world what they want to see
I think I'm better off being happy

Some people want fame
Some want lots of money
I just want my friends and family

To love someone, for eternity
Those are my dreams and they suit me.

Lauren Price (14)
Barnwood Park School

War Is Over

War is over
Kids are dying
Adults crying
Even when it's over I can still hear the banging of the drum
The gathering of guns

Still crying, I can hear
Crying of kids
Crying because they can't find their mums or dads
Everyone's gone
They have no one
Now the war is over.

Kayleigh Huntley (12)
Barnwood Park School

Equality

I have a dream to be equal
Many years ago, this was unheard of
Judged by your colour
Instead of how you treat others
The past makes me sad
Because we were never equal

Many tried to abolish it
But they always tried and failed
Many looked down on them
Many called them names
The past makes me sad
Because we were never the same

Many years later, many tried to abolish it
And this time they tried and prevailed
So when you look at others
Do not call them names
Please do not mistrust others
Always treat them like your brothers.

Shakirat Adesanya (14)
Barnwood Park School

Bullying

I have a dream about bullying
It is something I dream of all the time
Inside I feel loads of anger
Is this really happening or is just a dream?

My brother is always being bullied
He feels sad and lonely
I try to cuddle up to him
But he is always pushing me away

I say to him I love him so
But he never listens to me anymore
I just wish this dream will go
Because I love him loads.

Sophie Meadows (13)
Barnwood Park School

I Have A Dream

I have a dream to be a dancer
And everybody else would watch
I dance on my toes I'll dance on my feet
While my parents listen to the rhythm of my beat

Spinning on my head
Jumping off my bed
Messing around
You won't hear any sound

My feet are so light
I practise in the night
I dance to the beat
I let off lots of heat

Now I am one of them
I could easily pass
Now I dance so neat
My test will be complete.

Laura Corrick (12)
Barnwood Park School

I Have A Dream

I have a dream to be a designer
For textiles it would be
Sofas, beds and furniture
For everyone to see

I'd make them multicoloured
Different styles too
Some would be silky covered
To make them all go woo!

Different styles for everyone
You can choose the best
You would have loads of fun
Orange, purple or even red.

Charlie Izatt (11)
Barnwood Park School

I Have A Dream

I have a dream to be a celebrity
To star in movies
I have a dream to be a horse rider
To gallop in the fields
I have a dream to own a zoo
To feed and mess around with
I have a dream to own loads of dogs
To mess around with all the time
I have a dream to be a beautician massager
To take all your worries away
I have a dream to own a spa treatment palace
To make you feel like you're in paradise
I have a dream to be a hairdresser
To put your hair in funky styles
I have a dream to dance
To tap on the stage
I have a dream to own a shop
To sell ice cream in the summer
I have a dream to be a teacher
To scrape my chalk on the whiteboard
I have a dream, a dream, a dream . . .

Shelby Hopkins (11)
Barnwood Park School

I Have A Dream

I dream to fly with the houses at my side
As I play in the wind with pride
I dream to fly like a bird in the sky
As I dream to take off and fly
I dream to fly with a nice soft breeze
As I look and start to get teased
I dream to fly like a bird swooping down
As I start to look like a clown.

Kirsty-Louise Hardy (11)
Barnwood Park School

I Have A Dream

I have a dream to become a writer
Like J K Rowling and write to the stars
I would write horror, fantasy, adventure
Or love and things that are just for laughs

I have a dream to work with horses
Like Zara Phillips and ride to the stars
I'd go through the golden doors and
Ride over the purple moors

I have a dream to be a policewoman
To work with my colleagues, to help other people
To catch all the villains
And lock them in jail

I have a dream to be a nurse and work in the SCBU
And help other people too!

I have a dream to be just like you!

Helen Overs (12)
Barnwood Park School

I Had A Dream

I had a dream that snakes could walk
Walk to the edge of the world
I had a dream that cows could dive
Dive to the Earth's crust
I had a dream that penguins could fly
Fly to a planet above
I had a dream that fish could run
Run in every race
I had a dream that owls could climb
Climb to the highest hill
I had a dream that I was happy . . .
And I knew that was true.

Chloe Riddick (11)
Barnwood Park School

My Dream!

I have a dream
To be a shopping machine
I would always go shopping
There's no time for stopping
Maybe in New York
I'll do a catwalk

My dream may come true
And I believe this too
I will make sure it happens
And for that I will
Rob a bank

I have a dream
To be a shopping machine
There's no time for stopping
Maybe in New York
I'll do a cat walk

I need a credit card
It may be very hard
Now I think I need a bodyguard!

Chloe Tonks (11)
Barnwood Park School

My Dream

D ance constantly on stage
A udience cheering while I dance
N othing will ever stop me!
C lapping, it's all I could hear, they love me!
I   stood in the spotlight
N obody will hate me, they will love me
G ems and rubies glistening!

Elizabeth Baber (12)
Barnwood Park School

I Have A Dream

I have a dream to be an artist
I would paint people and landscapes too
I would love to be the greatest
When I reveal all my pictures I see the crowd shouting woo

Oh how I would love to be an artist so
Thinking of all the lovely places I could go
Drawing my designs onto paper
Then painting them out in neat later

The person who inspires me is Rolf Harris
The perfect place to set up my studio would be in my garage
I would design things to paint
I would give some of my pictures to my mates

Mixing palettes all day long
When I'm painting I may burst into song
How I dream to be an artist
People will say I am the smartest

I would try my best every day
I would hold an art stall for people to pay

Oh how I would love to be an artist so
I would always be happy and never in woe
I would take time in all my paintings
When I paint I may have to do a lot of waiting
Although it may take a lot of time
I would spend on it all my pride

My paintings would make other people smile
When I see this I know it would be worth my while.

Victoria Cooper (12)
Barnwood Park School

I Have A Dream

I have a dream to be a star
Sitting in my flashy car
In my house upon a hill
My shiny armoured knight called Bill
Being followed by a camera man
Being chased all day by my favourite fan
Eating posh food all day long
Smelly cheese that don't half pong!

I dream to be a princess
I dream to be a queen
I dream to meet a handsome knight
The best I've ever seen
Slaying dragons left to right
Through the day and all the night
One I know who will be king
When fish do swim and birds do sing

I dream to be me
I dream to be you;
I dream to be everything at the zoo;
I am a vegetarian
And I'm a carnivore

The first and second just aren't true,
But all my life . . .
I'll be with you.

Leanne Rutledge & Rosie Evans (13)
Barnwood Park School

Amy

Amy
Your smiling face
Is as gorgeous as lace
You smile your one tooth smile
When I see you in the morning
You make my life worthwhile
When you are sleepy I hold you close
And hug you tight
Snuggling you for all of the night
And if you cry
I won't lie and say that I am busy
When you've done a wizzy
I stroke my fingers through your hair
As you drift off without a care
I had a dream to make everyone smile
And you have done this by a mile
I love you with all my heart
You have given this family a new start.

Georgia Ellmore (12)
Barnwood Park School

I Have A Dream

I have a dream
I dream to fly high up in the sky
Just like a fly
Passing all the bugs by

I want to be a teacher
Because I like all children (or do I?)
Then I can cast a spell
In my magic cauldron

I wish, I wish for it to come true
It needs to be real
Shake hands on it
It's a deal!

Katie Clutterbuck (12)
Barnwood Park School

A Dream

A journey through a parallel world
Drifting without pain or desire
Floating through the unknown
Travelling in a haze of fire
Did I have a dream
Or did the dream have me?

A secret still untold
A mystery still unsolved
A swirling whirlwind that takes a hold
A beautiful nightmare that takes control
Did I have a dream
Or did the dream have me?

A transitory wander through unbroken
A mirror image of a life
Possessing an emotion unexplained
Possessing a title never named
Did I have a dream
Or did the dream have me?

Carrie Talbot (13)
Barnwood Park School

I Have A Dream

I have a dream to climb the highest mountain
And land in the most poshest fountain

I have a dream to own a zoo
Or live on a farm with the cows saying, 'moo.'

I have a dream to be a millionaire
Or even a billionaire

I have a dream to live on a boat
Or live in a castle with a big moat

I have a dream to be on the telly
Where all my dreams are from.

Jess Hollyhead (11)
Barnwood Park School

I Had A Dream

I had a dream that I was very bold I won the gold in the Olympic games
My very high aims got no fame and my dreams were famous too
Some of my dreams are high but some are low and I never let them go
This one is here to stay I'm never letting my chance slip away.

My idol is my sister, she's fast, she's bold and she's also 14 years old
She great at sports all different sorts
And she has a sports captain badge
My dream will come true if I just believe
A gold medal is the prize I will receive.

Poppy Thompson (11)
Barnwood Park School

I Have A Dream!

I have a dream of being the ocean
Not living with commotion
My hair is soft and wavy like a petal
And will never settle
My face is graceful like a dove,
With so much love
But my body is what you desire
This is my dream
So
Don't
Let
It
Wash
Away
Into
The
Distance.

Lauren Dickson (11)
Barnwood Park School

I Have A Dream . . .

I have a dream to live abroad
In the hot, boiling sun
A big house, a swimming pool
Where I can swim and have some fun

My mum inspired me
To live abroad
There's lots of entertainment
And you never get bored

I have a dream to be a physiotherapist
So I can take away the pain
Then the unhappiness of people
Will flow away down the drain

I wish, I wonder
Will it be true
I want it to be real
I really do.

Hollie Jones (12)
Barnwood Park School

I Dream Of Being A Dancer

D ancing queen
A crowd is clapping
N ice, nice dancer
C lapping is all I can hear
I   try my best
N o one is better
G reat, great, great.

Katy Mace (11)
Barnwood Park School

I Have A Dream

I walk on my toes
In a hip hop sort of way
I wiggle and I wriggle
As I walk and as I play

Dancing is the start for me
And as I walk it follows me
Down the street I feel the beat
But never relying on my own feet

Dancing, dancing, comes first for me
Swimming, swimming comes second for me
As I walk I collect my fee
And as I dance it comes back to me

Dancing is the start for me
And as I walk it follows me
Down the street I feel the beat
But never relying on my own feet

As I dance I move my feet
And as I dance I feel the beat

Dancing is the start for me
And as I walk it follows me
Down the street I feel the beat
But never relying on my own feet.

Katie Harris (11)
Barnwood Park School

I Have A Dream

I have a dream to own millions of shoes
This helps me to beat the blues
I like sparkles, black, high or low
Leather, fabric, buckle or bow
All shapes and sizes
Sales, bargains are my prizes

Hollywood, London, Paris and Tokyo
I'm going shopping, let's go, go, go!
Whatever the cost
I'll never get lost
As long as I've got my shoes

I'm sure I'll make it there
I'd do it for a dare
Then I'd find I like it
And do it when I want it
I'd shop all day and night
And when I wear them I feel bright
When I have some shoes!

My inspirations are the models of this world
They're young, flexy and very curled
I'd love to look like them
I'd have all eyes on me
And I will be
The best!

Laura Stokes (11)
Barnwood Park School

I Have A Dream . . .

I have a dream to own a pink sporty car
I'm glad it's not black or it would look just like tar

I like shoes, all shapes and sizes
I'm glad the sale is on then I will get great surprises

I like clothes, jeans, tops - strapless or v-neck
I shop for them everywhere, somewhere like Next

I need a car to go very far
I need shoes to beat the blues
I need clothes to look like a pro

In my pink sporty car
Hoping to go out with Lemar

My big high stilettos
Trying not to show my toes

My jeans and v-neck or strapless tops
I look like someone who hiphops!

I need a car to go very far
I need shoes to beat the blues
I need clothes to look like a pro.

Carlie Baker (12)
Barnwood Park School

I Have A Dream

I have a dream
Good for you
I dream when I'm sad
I dream when I'm good
I dream about you

I have a dream
It's you
My only friend
I dream of us being together
When the skies go blue
I dream of you

I dream the world of you
Be with me, make me happy
Let my dream come true
Let it be you all the time
When my dreams come so blue
Makes me want to be with you

I have a dream
To be with you
Let it come true.

Amanda Bennett (15)
Barnwood Park School

I Have A Dream . . .

I have a dream
To be a millionaire
So I can make all the boys stare

I have a dream
To live abroad
Somewhere hot
And sunbathe on a golden beach

My mum inspired me
To become famous
And meet all the other
Famous people

I have a dream
To live in a big house
And have a personal driver
To drive me around in my
Sparkling clean, white limo

I have a dream
To travel the world
Reaching the strangest
Places of all

I have a dream
That all this will come true
Hoping and wishing
That my life
Won't turn blue.

Melanie Clement (12)
Barnwood Park School

I Have A Dream

I have a dream
To explore the world
I have a dream
To spend my life with you

When things go wrong
I have a dream
I have a dream about you and smile
Let me dream, let me
Have a wonderful dream
About you

You mean the world to me
Everything about you keeps me stuck in time
I watch you, I gaze at you, I smile at you
I have a dream
That is to explore the world with you

I have a dream
To be with you
I have a dream
To stay with you
When my dreams become so blue
I think of you
And become one with you.

Katriona Stuart (14)
Barnwood Park School

My Nursing Dream

I have a dream to be a nurse
To look after children and babies
To help them through rough and tough
And make sure they don't get rabies

They can also catch chickenpox and flu
MRSA and cancer too
So I make sure they stay healthy and well
So they grow up fit and nobody can tell

I watch Casualty and Holby City
And one day hope to join the hospital committee
They inspired me to become a nurse
And make sure people don't get hurt

I'll go on the ward feeling happy and chilled
And come off proud 'cause nobody got killed
I'd love my job more than any other
And everyone will be proud including my father and mother.

Amy Garbett (12)
Barnwood Park School

I Have A Dream

I have a dream to be a dancer
Who wears pink all the time
I would be the best ballet, prancer
And would get away with crime

I have a dream to be a singer
Who could sing splendid and merry
I would have money wrapped around my finger
I would be better than Mariah Carey

I have a dream to be a beautician
Who makes everyone look pretty
Then I would go on a big mission
And do the whole of the city

I have a dream to be a gymnast
Who is flexible and bright
Then I can get to the top fast
And will shimmer through the night.

Philisha Tyne (12)
Barnwood Park School

I Love My Family

I dream one day far away I meet my handsome prince
He glistens in the morning, he shines at night
That's my dream

I dream I have a family happy as can be
With two children and he who's meant to be
That's my dream

I dream we will be together forever, just us four
That's my dream

I dream we will walk the roads holding close together
That's my dream

I dream I'll never let you fade or go
I hope you'll always be here with us
That's my dream

I dream, I dream, I dream.

Tammy Hiam (11)
Barnwood Park School

Dancer

D reaming of fame
A   stage with me on it
N o one but me
C lapping all I can hear, they love me
E nergetically in the spotlight
R ings and jewellery on me.

Laura Bevan (11)
Barnwood Park School

If Only . . .

My heart's all a flutter
Melting like butter
The boy of my dreams I see
Is sleeping soundly under the apple tree
If only . . .

In the field of flowers
Colours swirl round and round
Lively sheep are running abound
If only . . .

The scent of flowers
Engulf me in an aroma of honeysuckle
Dazzling daisies are floating about my chin
Making me chuckle
If only . . .

The boy awakes, we laugh and dance
He can't keep up with me
He has no chance
If only . . .

Suddenly I awake
The sound of city police cars ringing in my ears
It was just a dream, my eyes fill with tears
Outside the window my dream boy stands
Pale and sad with fags in his hands

If only my dream would one day come true
I'm sure life would be worth living
I know that much is true.

Abbie Phillips (14)
Barnwood Park School

Dreams For A Perfect World

We all can choose how our lives turn out,
Not the ones that people are about.

People create problems they cannot sort,
Is it time that we in our dreams abort?

We have our visions, we have our thoughts,
We have our rights, we have our hopes.

We have the feelings, we all have a doubt,
That there's a thing we can't live without.

That can be freedom that can be peace,
That can be the thing we desire.

Everyone knows what this is about
We all can choose how our lives turn out.

Jonathan Carr (13)
Belmont Special Needs School

I Have A Dream

I have a dream that when I am grown,
I will travel the world when I leave home.

I'll travel high and travel low,
I'll learn many things,
Along the way as I go.

I will comfort the sick
And I'll help the poor,
I'll work and I'll toil
And do so much more.

My dream is to greet,
Everyone that I meet,
With a smile and a helping hand.

We'll all be together,
Through storm and bad weather,
Together as one, we will stand.

Alex Gibbons (12)
Belmont Special Needs School

I Have A Dream

We should choose the way we want to live,
Not how people tell us how to live.

We've got rights to love and give,
People have rights to their dreams.

We have our rights to eat the things we eat,
We have our rights to a world we like,
With no more chores - which is a total bore.

We have our rights to a world,
With no more school - which would be cool.

We have our rights to a world with no more litter,
We have our rights to no more winter which is bitter.

We have our rights to no more endless poverty,
We have our rights to love and care,
We have our rights to share.

Kirstie Grainger (14)
Belmont Special Needs School

I Have A Dream

I want to be a big tall tree,
A cat perhaps or a bumblebee.

I want a fairy who will give me a wish,
Of better things to come.

I would spend my days in different ways
And imagine what I could become.

The road may be long,
But I am strong
And I'll follow my dream to the end.

Sylvia Aboagye (12)
Belmont Special Needs School

I Have A Dream

My dream would be for harmony,
With everyone I meet,
We would help each other along life's way,
Not just once but every day,
Could this work this dream of mine?
I will only know in the fullness of time.

Michael Tilling (15)
Belmont Special Needs School

Untitled

White face, black face join together,
Blue eyes, brown eyes join together,
Grey hair, blonde hair join together.

Poor family, rich family join together,
Clean clothes, dirty clothes join together,
Big house, small house join together.

No matter how you look,
No matter if you're cool,
Join together, stop the hate,
Together we will rule.

George Grindle (13)
Heywood Community School

My Dreams

My dream is to play for the great British Lions,
I would be better than the best,
It is like a knighthood, only better,
It is as real as life,
As plain as day,
As unique as the last animal on Earth,
My dream is my inspiration,
My heart would be a shooting star if my dreams came true.

Matthew Hawkins (12)
Heywood Community School

I Have A Dream

I have a dream that the world could be free of racial discrimination,
Where the whole world could get along, where all colours
are accepted,
That all colours could come together in harmony and share the world,
That people are proud to be what they are and respected for it,
I have a dream that the world would be like this.

Heidi Beddington (12)
Heywood Community School

I Have A Dream

I have a dream that the world is a great place to live,
With nice people and there is nothing to be afraid of,
I have a dream that no one needs to fight or argue
And we all get along and we have a great, caring loving family,
I have a dream that the world is a better and brighter, friendlier
place to be.

Shannon Roberts (12)
Heywood Community School

I Have A Dream

D reams running through my head,
R ealising things in life through my sleep,
E ntertaining dreams or sad, funny or mad,
A ll people take part just like real life,
M y head thinks things I want to come true,
S howing what I want to happen in life.

It goes on for a while but then it dies off,
It's time for real life again.

Sophie Coombs (13)
Heywood Community School

This Love

I dream of having a kiss like an ocean of love coming to my lips,
I dream of a voice that is a soft whisper in my ear,
I dream of a hand touching my skin just like a delicate spiderweb,
I dream of a smile that shines like the sun,
I dream of having skin as soft as a velvet cloth, colourful and rich,
I dream of having a life like a princess, flowing dresses and rosy lips,
All the white doves to show love and kind,
Waiting to be taken off my feet by a prince.

He has a kiss like an ocean of love,
He has a voice like a soft whisper,
He has a hand that touches my skin, delicate spider's web,
He has a smile like a shining sun,
He has skin as soft as a rich, colourful velvet cloth,
He swept me off my feet, just treated me like a princess.

I dreamt of the day he'd love me. He now does.

Nikola Michelle Price (14)
Heywood Community School

Dreams

I have a dream,
To become famous,
To live in a house as big as a palace
And have a wardrobe as big as a cottage,
To go to award shows and walk down the
Red carpet with everyone shouting and
Calling my name,
Big lights flashing,
Delighted faces cheering,
Going shopping with the stars to New York,
Then swim in my huge pool,
That's my dream,
All of my dreams are like endless tunnels.

Ellie Turner (11)
Heywood Community School

I Have A Dream . . .

To live life to the full,
To have no fear,
To not be afraid of anyone and anything.

I also dream . . .

Of a thing I see,
A thing that scares me,
A thing that would send shivers down
Anyone's back in different ways,
These dreams are not dreams, but nightmares.

To cure me from those nightmares . . .

Think of more joyful things,
Things that I would like,
Things that can raise a smile,
Things where no matter what happens,
I will always be happy . . .

Those are the dreams I want.

Claire Herbert (12)
Heywood Community School

I Have A Dream

I have a dream to go back to Disney World,
Arriving at the gates with a smile,
If dreams come true,
Wishes should too,
Because dreaming is wishing,
Is thinking,
Is hoping
And is believing.
Dreaming is like magic filling us with happiness and joy,
Dreaming is wishing your dreams would come true,
I have a dream that all my wishes and dreams come true.

Charlie Roberts (12)
Heywood Community School

Untitled

I dream of a world,
Where there is no pain or hurt,
When people have seen the problems
And they have learnt.

I dream of a world,
Where love is taken and given,
When people have seen the problems
And they have forgiven.

I dream of a world,
Where religion doesn't separate,
When people have seen the problems
And used it to build and create.

I dream of a world,
Where crime is no more,
When people have seen the problems
And have learnt to respect the law.

I dream of a world,
Where love is no longer burnt,
When people have seen the problems
And realise love is a price to be earnt.

I dream of a world,
Where a dreamer can dream,
When people have seen the problems
And respect the possibilities unseen.

Rebecca Green (15)
Heywood Community School

My Dreams - Haiku

I love to have dreams
They will always inspire me
Imagination.

Kate Baldwin (12)
Heywood Community School

My Dream

I have a dream in this world,
That all the hate will cease
And all of the human race,
Will just make peace.

I have a wish in this life,
That no one could ever be dead,
That way for millions of people,
There will be no more grieving or dread.

I get inspiration from
All the things around
Whether they might be up
High or on the ground.

We get our motivation,
From the weird and strange things,
Whether it be the Spice Girls
Or Martin Luther King.

Lilia Osborne (12)
Heywood Community School

I Have A Dream

I have a dream, I have a wish,
I dream and wish that I could live my imagination,
That life would be fine
And go in a straight line,
No problems to drive you round the bend
And make it seem there is no end.

I have a dream, I have a wish,
I dream and wish that nothing will go wrong,
Nothing to upset you or even make you cry,
That will never happen!

Oh why! Oh why! Oh why!

Sarah Jelf (12)
Heywood Community School

I Dream

I dream about the world being peaceful,
I dream about life being changed,
If my dream ever came true,
The world wouldn't have war or poverty,
No murder or hatred, it would definitely be changed,
Friends would stay friends, no arguments,
Or sorrow, but *how*?
People you care about would never go to hospital
Or get ill, they would always be happy and well,
The world has bad things,
So does life, but to deal with it you have to be brave,
My world and my life - will it change?

Natalie Bonser
Heywood Community School

Dream Poem

D is for the darkness that shouldn't be in people's hearts,
R is for the racism that should stop in the world,
E is for the endless hunger that happens in this life,
A is for all the arguments I wish I could stop,
M is for the marriages that started with love and ended in hate.

Is this what the world should be?
You may only be one person,
But fulfilling just one dream,
You could make this one world,
One better place to be.

Katie Weatherley (12)
Heywood Community School

I Have A Dream

P erhaps the world could be different,
E verything, everybody changed, no one,
R emembering what it is like now,
F ighting, discrimination and racism,
E verywhere, pain and suffering, it
C ould vanish, everyone could come
T ogether and try to make the

W orld a better place just imagine,
O r believe in something, you could
R ecreate the world. You could change
L ives of millions, with power, a
D ream could become reality, not just a thought.

Izzie Gazzard (13)
Heywood Community School

I Have A Dream . . .

I have a dream . . .
N eath Swansea Ospreys is the team
S mashing and mashing,
P ulvarising other teams,
I nterested in every aspect of the game,
R ugby is never lame,
A nnihilating is so fun,
T ackling can injure them,
I nvolvement is the only way you can win,
O n the ball every time,
N ever boring, never lame, rugby is the greatest ever game!

Billy Head (12)
Heywood Community School

I Have A Dream

I have a dream,
That one day we will all be friends,
One day we can make amends.

I have a dream,
That there will be no more fighting,
No more war and no more hating.

I have a dream,
That I can be free, see all the things
That I want to see.

I have a dream,
That life could be simple, no complications,
No worries or regrets.

Jenny Salter (13)
Heywood Community School

Dreams

Dreams,
The inspiration,
For generations,
The start of a great change.

Dreams,
Making a difference,
Sheep over the fence,
Challenging life itself.

Dreams,
The motivation,
From idolisation,
Making your dreams come true!

Dreams.

Joy Fellows (12)
Heywood Community School

Dream Of A World

Dream of a world,
That is peaceful,
That is green
And that is just.

Dream of a world,
With no war,
No pollution
And no evil.

Dream of a world,
That is loving,
That is fair
And equal.

Do you dream of this world?
Well don't dream, make,
Unite together and make a better world today.

Robert Elmer (12)
Heywood Community School

My Dream

M aking a dream when you go to sleep,
Y our dreams can be full of surprises,

D ecisions throughout, this way, that way,
R acism stops forever, never to be seen again,
E xcitement runs through your veins, stopping at every organ on
the way,

A dventures that change,
M eeting celebs and admirers you've always loved.

My dreams are like these, are yours?

Jordan Taylor (12)
Heywood Community School

My Dream

D iscrimination against different sexes, ages and races,
R acism against the other races,
E xploitation of the environment and the weak,
A buse against types of life,
M urder of animals and humans.

I dream of a world without prejudice, environment, the weak,
Abuse of power.
Discrimination, racism, exploitation,
Abuse and murder and many more.

I dream of a world with success where people exploit
People's potential,
Where the fighting stops and the peace starts,
Where two people can come together and not
Fight but think of something exciting not discriminating.

I dream of a world of happiness, success, potential,
Peace and excitement,
This doesn't have to be just a dream,
This can be now.

Jordan James (12)
Heywood Community School

I Have A Dream

I magine a world with no war or conflict,
M aking the world a better place
A place where people can live in peace,
G iving people back their lives,
I nvest in the world, not war,
N ever again, any more wars,
E nsure the world is a happy and peaceful place.

Lydia Holford (13)
Heywood Community School

Untitled

Dreams give us hope when no one else can,
Dreams help us to forgive when we can't,
Dreams take us into a world of fantasy
And when we wake up it's back to reality,
Dreams give us hope when no one else can.

Amelia Wheatstone (13)
Heywood Community School

I Have A Dream . . .

D reams are a wish but it may come true,
R acism should not be, all calm and peaceful,
E ach other should come together as one,
A nyone should be able to live in peace,
M ost people should be loved and have a better life.

Samantha Meek (12)
Heywood Community School

I Have A Dream

I have a dream
Of no discrimination: racial belief or any
                        other sort of inequality.

I have a dream
That everyone will cooperate, that poverty
And cruelty will be dispelled.

I have a dream
Of no wars, all nations together
United we stand . . .
Parted we fall,
I have a dream!

Jenny Forrester (12)
Newent Community School

I Have A Dream

What if,
We were all free?
What if,
No slavery?
What if,
The world forgave?
What if,
We were all brave?

What if,
We all got along?
What if,
We all grew up to be strong?
What if,
We all had food?
What if,
We were all in a good mood?

What if,
We were all friends?
What if,
We tied up loose ends?
What if,
Pain and hate were a thing of the past?
What if,
Everyone's life could last?

Erin Taylor (12)
Newent Community School

I Had A Dream

I went to sleep,
Eyes closed tight,
I dreamt of toys,
All through the night.

I slumbered through,
My dream so far,
A boat, a plane,
A big red car.

Someone whispered,
'Come this way,'
A sparkling room,
Like a sunshine ray.

Big ted, little ted,
All furry and brown,
I'm snugly, still dreaming,
Under my eiderdown.

Wow, lots of toys,
My eyes could see,
But it's time for breakfast,
My mum is calling me.

My dream must end,
My sparkling jewel,
My mum's just called,
Oh, it's time for school.

Sydney Foster (13)
Newent Community School

I Have A Dream

       I   have a dream

       H ealth to everyone
       A nd fish in a stream
The V ery poor, having fun
       E veryone should live my dream

       A nyone can live my dream

       D rinking water for all
       R eality won't make me lie
       E veryone needs a safety net when they fall
       A nother child in Africa dies
       M y dream is a powerful dream.

Nathaniel Barker (12)
Newent Community School

I Have A Dream

I have a dream,
It may be silly,
I would like a hamster,
I'd name it Billy.

I have a dream,
It may run riot,
To have a lion,
That won't keep quiet.

I have a dream,
However small it may be,
To at least own a pet,
That will look after me!

Lydia Buckley (11)
Newent Community School

Imagine A World

Imagine a world without child abuse,
Children could live safe in their homes,
Without worry, without panic,
Without the anxiety of being attacked.

Not frightened and not scared,
Not dreading the moment the door opens,
Without cries and screams
And no tears or fears.

Just being happy and smiling,
Cheerful and jolly,
Relaxed and calm
And the world would be a better place.

Jack Baker (11)
Newent Community School

I Have A Dream

I have a dream,
No more animal testing,
No more cruel bullying,
No more animal poaching,
No more cruel beatings.

I have a dream,
Everyone has healthy food,
Everyone has clean water,
Everyone has a healthy life,
Everyone has clean clothes.

I have a dream,
We all are happy,
We all help each other,
We all are joyful,
We all help the world.

Lewis Pritchard (12)
Newent Community School

I Have A Dream

In my world there is
Someone for everyone
And no one has to
Go it alone
Good friends are
Never too far away
And you are never too far from home.

        In my world there are
        Sparkling spiders' webs
        In the fresh morning
        Comes the new sun
        Snow-white light
        Catching on diamond threads
        Beauty surrounding everyone.

                In my world there is
                Enough for all of us
                And no one has to
                Go without
                Mountains are
                Never too high to climb
                And all you have to do is shout.

In my world there are
Tigers and panda bears
Gone from the zoos and
Surviving free
Bright stripes
A silhouette sunset there
I feel that my dream can never be.

        In my world there are
        Kids round a campfire
        And there is always
        Room for one more
        Thousands
        Warm their hands at the flames
        And we forget there was ever a law.

In my world there are
Snow-caps and deserts,
Rippling lakes,
Rolling green hills
Most of all
There is peace and harmony,
I know that my dream will not be fulfilled.

Miriam Vesma (12)
Newent Community School

I Have A Dream

Single voices in the crowd,
People strong, brave, proud,
Their words can change the world,
But words can be twisted,
Changed and curled.

All men are created equal,
Or so that's what they say,
So why are some made slaves,
To toil away all day?

If they unite together,
So much easier it will be,
If they work, pray and suffer together,
Then maybe they will see,
That creed and colour don't matter,
But love and friendship do
And maybe some day the whole world,
Will come to see this too.

Jay Timney (12)
Newent Community School

I Have A Dream

I have a dream,
One day there will be peace,
Across the whole nation,
Everyone will shake hands,
Between them create a new friendship.

I have a dream,
Every mountain, hill and valley,
Shall be transformed,
Into a magical, calm view,
Where everyone will learn,
The true meaning of life.

I have a dream,
The world,
Becomes a fair world,
That necessary things
Are accessible to everyone,
That luxuries,
Are shared evenly.

I have a dream,
Criminals, diseases,
The whole world becomes
A perfect harmony,
I have a dream,
Let my dream come true.

Elise Goulding (13)
Newent Community School

I Have A Dream

I have a dream
That people will live,
Live their lives to the full.
That every moment of happiness,
That can possibly be savoured,
Will be wrung of enjoyment.
That people's minds
Will be stacked with joyful memories,
Leaving no room for sadness and hate.
That people will do what they can
To bring a smile to someone's face
And make a stranger's day.
I have a dream,
That people will not spend their days
Sitting in the darkness, worrying
But will step into the light and smile.
There is no past,
It is gone,
There is no future,
To be sure of,
But there is now,
So grasp it tightly
And let yourself go!
I have a dream to live for now.

Lorna Baggett (13)
Newent Community School

I Have A Dream . . .

I have a dream that one day racial
Inequalities will be forgotten.
Racism is a big boulder growing amid
Small pebbles of hope.
Joining together will stamp out that darkness,
For racism is an enemy against who we must
Fight and eventually win.

I have a dream that we shall rise from the
Dark depths of arrogance
Fighting for justice, human rights and fair laws
That black and white people will both be
Judged by character not colour of skin
For racism is an enemy against who we must
Fight and eventually win.

Iain Docherty (13)
Newent Community School

I Have A Dream

I have a dream of sunny skies,
I have a dream of white flags,
No more wars,
No more deaths that could be avoided,
I dream that peace and harmony would break out,
That love would rule
And war would stop.

I have a dream that the world's heart will
Beat as one with ours,
The valley of friendship will be unveiled,
That one day life will begin and end with peace.

Julia Greenwood (13)
Newent Community School

I Have A Dream

I have a dream,
One day the Earth will be happy,
Not just a country,
But the Earth shall be happy,
One ant in a whole colony can make a
Difference,
Can you?

I have a dream,
That all people shall fight with words,
Not war,
Life is to be enjoyed,
One fish in the sea can make a difference,
Can you?

I have a dream,
Everyone should be accepted for who they are,
That the world will stand up to racism,
Not the colour of their skin,
One voice in a whole football crowd can
Make a difference,
Can you?

Will Jenkins (13)
Newent Community School

I Had A Dream

That there was a world with no diseases,
That there was a world where everyone had a home,
That there was a world without pollution,
That there was a world without anyone being kidnapped,
That there was a world where everyone had food and fresh water,
That there was a world without child abuse,
That there was a world without racial abuse.

Matthew Eastwood (11)
Newent Community School

I Have A Dream

I have a dream that one day natural disasters
Wouldn't strike so fiercely killing and leaving
People in pain.
I have a dream that black and white people could
Come together with peace and harmony
And walk off hand in hand against racism.
I have a dream that terrorism will stop and
People could be at peace with the world.
I have a dream that homelessness will become a
Thing of the past
And starvation would no longer be
And everyone could sit down to food and eat
Meals every day.
I have a dream that wars will stop and the
World will become fresh and peachy
And all countries will be able to stand up to
Freedom together and with each other.
All abuse, fighting and bullying will not
Become an every day thing but never again.
I have a dream.

Clare Kerr (13)
Newent Community School

I Have A Dream

Imagine a whole world without child abuse,
Where they can play happily,
Where children can go home without worrying,
What will happen?
The happiness that would be in every child's eyes,
All the love and life in the children as they play,
The fun in them near holidays,
Christmas and Easter,
But imagining is all we can do.

Carolyn Quinn (12)
Newent Community School

I Have A Dream!

I have a dream,
A dream that the world can be free from racism,
Prejudice and war.
A dream that people can stand hand in hand,
As equals.
A dream that people should not live in fear,
But shine and be who they really are.
A dream that people whose mouths are
Dripping with the words of crime and injustice
Are wiped clean
And that everyone can achieve their ambitions,
Their dreams.
I have a dream today,
Joined together in peace,
Our world is a better place.

Anna Charlesworth (13)
Newent Community School

Life Is Precious

Life is precious and precious is all,
Precious is living and precious is pure.
Life is for the living and not just for show,
Keep living your life and let everyone know.

People are dying of hunger and thirst,
While people are living on other people's work.
People have everything, but are still feeling low,
Keep living your life and let everyone know.

Pleasure is knowing what you can do,
Not knowing that others are worse off than you.
Pleasure is doing your best and to show,
Keep living your life and let everyone know.

Ben Norman (12)
Newent Community School

I Have A Dream!

I have a dream,
To be a superstar,
To sing and dance,
To lots of people
And perform to the world.

I have a dream,
That life is sweet,
As sweet as sugar,
Everything nice,
Everything easy.

I have a dream,
That the cities are clean,
The streets immaculate,
Nowhere is dirty,
Nowhere is scattered with litter.

I have a dream,
That people are friendly,
People are kind,
Everyone accepts each other.

I have a nightmare,
That the world is *racist,*
Everyone's selfish,
The world contains,
Unkind people!

But . . . then I have a dream,
That my family and I,
Have a happy future,
We live safe and calm,
Together, with each other.

Emily Suckling (12)
Newent Community School

I Have A Dream

One day, far away,
I can see a time,
That all cancers can be cured,
But is it down the line?

That all children,
Young and old,
Can remember Mum and Dad,
All the bad times, all the good,
That they ever had.

That mums and dads,
Can be sure,
That their precious children,
Will outlive them, not the other,
Because it can be the saddest thing ever.

That unlike me,
You can live,
With both parents by your side,
Them helping you through childhood
And you not see one die.

That you can smile,
You can laugh,
With no worries in the world,
About cancer cells coming
And ruining your world.

I wish, one day,
There will be a time,
That all cancers can be cured,
I hope it's down the line.

Danielle Trevail (12)
Newent Community School

I Had A Dream

I had a dream of a peaceful
World with no war or violence,
I had a dream where there was no famine and food for all.

I had a dream when a word could make a difference,
I had a dream of a loving world that cares for everyone.

I had a dream where no one was judged,
I had a dream with no racist remarks,
I had a dream that everyone was friends,
I had a dream with no drugs for bad use.

I had a dream that everyone was equal,
No terrorists or muggers or thieves,
I had a dream where everyone had a say,
Whether male or female.

I had a dream when animals weren't hunted,
I had a dream with no disease to get in our way.

I had a dream with a perfect world,
I had a dream where everyone had a chance.

I had a dream!

Matthew Wathen (11)
Newent Community School

Depression

I have a dream

Imagine a world without depression,
Imagine a world without pain,
Imagine children not weeping so much
And being so depressed and afraid.

Imagine a world where people didn't wish to kill themselves,
To ease the terrible sadness,
The sadness of tears
And the horrible nightmarish madness.

Sam Owen (12)
Newent Community School

I Have A Dream

I have a dream,
But fear the words of scorn and fun,
Because I want to be the one,
Who stands out from the crowd
And shouts out loud!

I have a dream,
To make a change,
To change the world from poverty,
I want to make a difference every day
And make people listen to my words.

I have a dream,
To help the world,
To clean it of disease
And stop all the thieves,
But what do you think?
Do you have a dream?

Charlotte Rimmer (12)
Newent Community School

Famine

The children are silent,
The tears we no longer see,
A face withdrawn and motionless,
As a mother stretches her arms out in plea.

A few grains of rice is all they need,
To help them through the day,
But there is not enough for all,
As the lorries turn and go away.

They only want to live happily,
As all should do,
They should have peace and harmony,
Just like me and you.

Jack Davis (11)
Newent Community School

I Once Had A Nightmare

I once had a nightmare
That the world was a living hell
Where people didn't care
Whether others were left to dwell.

Leaders were talking
Rivers of lies
For fear of
Guerrillas, terrorists and spies.

Spending money on weapons
For unwritten wars
Where only violence
Is used to settle scores.

I once had a nightmare
That the world was a living hell
Where people didn't care
Whether others were left to dwell.

Things were taken for granted
And people thrived in abundance
Whilst others received very little
And were very near redundant.

Many were discriminated
For their appearance or religion
They should treat everyone equally
But don't make that decision.

I once had a nightmare
That the world was a living hell
That people didn't care
Whether others were left to dwell.

Nature was being destroyed
The world was choking to death
We were edging nearer and nearer
To breathing our final breath.

I once had a nightmare
Though it was a shock for it would seem
That had I not woken up
For I was living the dream!

Sarah Granville (13)
Newent Community School

I Have A Dream

Life is a circle,
A circle of life,
Everyone stuck on this wheel,
Of dreams, of love, of hate, of envy,
Everyone is stuck right here.

Wouldn't it be lovely,
A world with no hunger,
No thirst and no pain,
A world that is just perfect,
In each and every way.

I've dreamt of a world,
Of friendship and care,
Where everyone knew freedom,
A freedom of speech,
A freedom of life,
A secret sanctuary from everywhere.

What if you could just leap off the wheel,
Into a paradise place,
Into a dreamworld,
A dream of all dreams,
This would be a dream of all dreams.

Emily Sladen (13)
Newent Community School

Down With Racism

I have a dream

If we all lived in England we would be white,
If we all lived in Africa we would be tanned,
If we all continue like we are,
From having a full life we will be banned.

Imagine a time in the future,
When instead of a racist remark,
They ask the boy to come and play,
Football in the park.

Waiting for the child,
Waiting just outside,
Instead of waiting to beat him,
Waiting to be kind.

Alex Bayross (11)
Newent Community School

Amnesty

I
Had
A dream
When I
Was young,
A glimpse of
Water and food
For all. I saw
Hope for people in
Africa and places
Where education is
Poor. I dream there
Is a place where
Everyone can
Be happy
And live together.
Heaven!

Elisabeth Fish (11)
Newent Community School

Inspirational Poem

I have a dream
'Stop bear baiting now.'

In a matter of weeks I will be mad,
But I shall tell you something sad,
I was ripped from my mother at the age of one,
Now I dance in the hot sun.

I took him as a cub some years ago,
Now I make him dance to and fro,
I chain him to stop him biting
And chop his claws to stop a deadly swipe.

I think of what I could have had,
To see my mother again, that would make me glad,
Running in the field, catching fish,
That is my desired wish.

Louise Morrisson (11)
Newent Community School

I Have A Dream

I have a dream that everyone has what they need,
That they have water,
Food,
Health.
I have a dream that everyone is happy,
That they spend time as a family,
Laugh and
Play.
I have a dream that there is no violence,
Racism,
Bullying
Or wars.

I have a dream!

Luke Kavallares (12)
Newent Community School

Inspirational Poem

I had a dream to stop all child abuse

I had a dream . . .
To help a child,
To stop a nightmare
And to start a life.

'Ouch!' a child would scream,
The abuse I can feel,
No one to help them
And no one to be seen.

Think,
Of a dark room,
No family to have,
Just a small child crying for help.

Why can't we help them?
Why can't we see,
The horror these children have,
All alone trying to sleep?

Think,
Of having a home,
With the worry,
Your siblings may be seized.

Think,
Of a time where there is no abuse,
Screams that you no longer hear,
Thinking of leaving that all behind.

Rachel Egan (12)
Newent Community School

I Have A Dream

I have a dream,
That everyone will get along,
That everyone is happy,
That people will not do wrong.

I have a dream,
That everyone is in perfect health,
That the poor will not be homeless
And the rich will share their wealth.

I have a dream,
That racism does not exist
And that war is not an issue,
It will not be missed.

I have a dream,
That poverty is no more,
That we can live in peace,
That there's no such thing as war.

I have a dream,
That everything is free,
That there are no robberies
And people can be what they want to be.

That was my dream,
I hope one day it will come true,
So the world can be a different place,
Fit for me and you.

Bethany Murray (12)
Newent Community School

I Have A Dream

Helping the homeless

Homeless people are in the street,
Being trodden on by people's feet,
A cardboard box is what they call home,
For food they fight over a bone.

They beg for money on their knees,
But they smell too much of mud and cheese,
But give them a home, they'll be alright,
They'll have a place to sleep at night.

They'll have a hot meal,
They won't be cold,
They'll have a bath
And scrub off the mould.

They'll have clean clothes,
They'll have some money,
They'll get a job
And smell as sweet as honey.

Alex Rann (12)
Newent Community School

Imagine A Time . . .

Imagine a time
When the bully isn't here,
Isn't there,
Not hitting or punching,
Small kids into submission.
He doesn't move on,
One after another,
To hurt and spread more
Fear and misery.
When the bully
Does care, does feel guilt,
There will be a time
When there is no hurt,
No fear of the outside,
When small kids
Can venture further than
Their front door and still
Feel safe.

Sam Goulding (12)
Newent Community School

I Had A Dream

I wish all children could be happy,
At school and at home,
To be able to walk to school alone,
To have a head as hard as stone.

If they were happy they would
Be playing with their friends,
Wouldn't it be nice to stop all bullying,
Children's bones are not supposed to bend.

I wish no kicking or hitting happened
And children had lots of friends,
No stealing of dinner money,
That they're just going to spend.

I wish that children never thought of bullying,
To play nicely all the time,
People who bully should be locked up,
They should feel as sour as a lime.

I sit at home and think,
People all over the world are scared and lonely,
Scared to go outside or look out the window,
The bully's head must be as big as a pony.

Philippa Maile (11)
Newent Community School

I Had A Dream . . .

To stop child cruelty

I had a dream to save the world,
To stop all children's pain,
My dream was big, I cannot deny,
Yet I still care so much, no little will I stop.

His arms are bruised,
His ankles are raw,
Then he speeds to the door,
My father shouts,
'Ow!'

Imagine a world with,
No children's pain,
My dreams came true,
To know you care so much.

His arms are fine,
His ankles good,
He walks out the door,
He's free.

Imagine and be happy.

Stopping child abuse is one of the main things
Causing pain to children in the world.

Verity Moulder (12)
Newent Community School

A Captured Dream

I had a dream,
It was a summer's day,
I was riding my bike
And off to play.

I passed colourful flowers,
I passed green trees,
The wind was in my hair,
Buzz went the bees.

The skies turned grey
And I fell off my bike,
The trees were snapped
And I fell off my bike.

I was in the future,
With pollution everywhere,
Global warming killed us,
The whole world was bare.

I was on my own,
So I walked around,
I found some magic seeds,
Which I planted in the ground.

The grass suddenly grew,
Colourful flowers too,
The wind was in my hair,
The sky was baby-blue.

I'd changed the future
And so can you,
It won't be hard,
Now you know what to do.

The sun was shining
And I was riding my bike,
It was a beautiful day,
Just a dream if you like!

Sophie Banyard (13)
Newent Community School

I Had A Dream

If only the world was war-free,
Hunger and poverty taken away,
A homeless woman with a life like me,
No one deserves poverty.

Children all safe at home,
Sat on the sofa drinking tea,
Used to be scared, all alone,
No one deserves poverty.

Money for food, drink and medicine,
Doctors and health carers always there for me,
A life filled with love and care,
No one deserves poverty.

Going to school with my friend,
No parents at home but
Life does not end,
No one deserves poverty.

A roof over my head,
A comfy, warm bed,
Asleep with my family,
No one deserves poverty.

Black or white,
Now school better than home,
It's horrid outside, on your own at night,
No one deserves poverty!

Rachel Dunn (12)
Newent Community School

Inspirational Poem

Imagine a world without poverty,
Food on everyone's plate,
Without illnesses to worry about
And fresh clothes to wear.

People in the Third World,
Not suffering, not struggling,
Places to sleep at night,
Keeping warm.

Enough money to pay for medicines
And a healthy lifestyle,
Children playing with their friends,
Thinking happy thoughts.

Nearby water stations,
Not wasting energy,
Money to teach children,
Writing and reading.

Imagine a world without poverty,
Living a happy life.

Sarah Parsons (12)
Newent Community School

I Have A Vision

I have a vision,
Of Guantanamo empty,
Of no more pain,
Behind its gates,
Of no more cramped cells,
Of no more visions of pain.

Of no more soldiers patrolling around it,
Of no more dodging human rights,
Of no more inhumane acts,
Of no more violence, cruelty, neglect,
No more, no more.

Of people getting fair trials,
Decent sized cells,
Men being treated like men,
Human rights being taken seriously,
No more need for iron bars,
That is my vision.

Felix Bartlett (11)
Newent Community School

I Have A Dream

I have a dream,
When our world works as one,
When people are not judged by their colour
And all can have fun.

I have a dream,
Where all animals can live,
When we don't torture them
And all we do is give.

I have a dream,
To help save the countries,
To cure all the illnesses,
Including cancer diseases.

I have a dream,
To help world hunger,
So that all can eat,
Even from a fishmonger.

I have a dream,
All countries will unite,
So all will be right.

Julia Tweedie (11)
Newent Community School

I Have A Dream

All kids are now safe,
No more bullying,
No more abuse,
All safe.

No more whipping,
No more starving,
No more stealing their money,
All kids are safe.

Everybody has the right to be treated the same,
It doesn't matter if you're black or white,
We all are special in a way,
We should be treated fair every day.

So before you go to hurt someone,
Or steal some money,
Think, put yourself in their shoes,
I don't like this, you shouldn't either.

Laiken Bennett (12)
Newent Community School

Inspiration Poem

I had a dream . . .
About child abuse.

I had a dream,
About child abuse,
To stop and end it, so it can be seen,
Like it has never happened.

I dreamt
That all the children's pain was over,
Like it was never there,
Now a child's happy,
Not sitting crying on the stair.

I dreamt
That everything that could have been done,
Has been done,
Now my stress has gone,
My head doesn't weigh a ton.

Olivia Powell (12)
Newent Community School

I Have A Dream

Listen, can you see a child's scream?
A child's hope?
Listen can you see
A step forward into life?
Where happiness is kind,
No wounds, no scrapes,
No bloody cuts,
Memories turn,
So they are happy again.

Imagine and feel an awful hurt,
A longing to help,
Imagine and feel a light in the dark,
Dreams become real,
No bruises or showing,
No lumps on your head,
Night turns to day,
Is happiness a cure to everything?
Imagine again a world -
A peaceful world.

Martha Wright (11)
Newent Community School

We Care

I have a dream -

Poverty doesn't make you grin,
Poverty isn't the way to win,
Poverty makes you frown,
Poverty makes everyone down.

Poverty takes so many lives a day,
We'll fight it, there must be a way,
Poverty is a global scare,
We'll fight it because we care.

Poverty doesn't make you grin,
Poverty isn't the way to win,
Poverty makes you frown,
Poverty makes everyone down.

Poverty is growing every day,
We'll fight it; there must be a way,
Poverty is real, it is there,
We'll fight it because we care.

Rob Penny (12)
Newent Community School

I Have A Dream

Imagine a world in 30 years,
With blistering heat, uncontrollable tears,
An ozone layer that's only a half,
The rarest thing on Earth will be a child's laugh,
Of all of the life that we're living today,
The desert and fear are here to stay.

A future like this we are able to stop,
If the cause will be taken, right to the top,
Global warming will soon go at last,
If selling fossil fuels is a thing of the past
And factories of evil,
Are free of deceival. Imagine.

The ozone layer is whole,
Without burning coal,
The Earth has the trees,
The birds and the bees,
A life that's worth living,
By saving the Earth, the Earth does its giving.

Wednesday Batchelor (12)
Newent Community School

I Have A Dream

I have a dream
A dream of a wonderful world,
Where the hand of friendship has no colour
And the cruelty of everyone, washed away.

I have a dream
Of a breathtaking world,
Where race doesn't matter
And colour isn't seen.

I have a dream,
Of a beautiful world,
Where hunger is no more
And we live in peace.

I had a dream
But it won't come true,
The world is too rigid
And that's the truth.

Charlotte Hickling (12)
Newent Community School

I Have A Dream

A dream is something they say comes true,
A dream is something for me and for you,
Many dreams have been seen,
Many dreams have been heard,
But many are secrets,
Hidden from the world.

I have dreams for lots of things,
World peace, animals, poverty and starvation,
I dream that a cure will be found for cancer,
I dream that my friends will find peace in their hearts.

But none of these dreams can come true without help,
People make these things happen,
If you have a dream,
Do something about it,
If you have a dream,
You can make it happen.

Laura Price (13)
Newent Community School

I Have A Dream

I have a dream,
But one person can't make a difference,
Can they?
Just one drop in the ocean,
Just one bird in the sky,
Just one.

Martin Luther King,
Just one,
He stood up,
He spoke out,
Changed the world,
Just one,
To gain respect,
To have no fear,
To have a dream.

Ellen McArthur,
Just one,
She climbed the mountain of water,
She broke the record,
Made history,
Just one,
To be a woman,
To conquer fears,
To have a dream.

Bob Geldof,
Just one,
He raised awareness and money,
He broke the mould,
Changed opinion,
Just one,
To be charitable,
To help others,
To have a dream.

I have a dream
And one person *can* make a difference,
They can,
Just one drop in the ocean,
Just one bird in the sky,
Just one!

Billie Arnold (13)
Newent Community School

I Have A Dream

As I step into my dream,
A world dances before me,
Mountains rise far in the distance
And fields of buttercups bloom.

And as I draw close,
Silence seems to shatter,
Giggling is heard throughout,
Small faces peep through the flowers.

And as if they were one big family,
Children of every colour,
With smiles on each of their beautiful faces,
Hold hands and form a circle.

Clamour echoes through the blue,
Reality dawns,
Brother shouts,
Sister screams.

Just a dream.

Issi Chamberlayne (13)
Newent Community School

I Have A Dream

Why do the trees with lush large greenery seem
To fall from the sky for all eternity?
Squawks and squeaks as they crash to the
Ground, tall trees? Never to be found.
Tropical birds must flee from their homes a
Flourish of fabulous feathers all they can see,
Searching for their young as creeps forth
The massive machinery.

I have a dream related to this a cousin,
A friend, an opposite.
My dream will change the world for the better,
Make it shine with all the glory of which it has stood,
I will tell you my dream, which I believe in,
It's so simple but leaves me longing, hanging
Suspended above thin air.

My dream is that trees will not fall yet stand proud and tall,
That machinery will not roam the rainforests
Yet rust away in darkness.
That birds and beasts as humans will not need to
Flee from greed and hatred hurriedly,
Nor slowly or indeed unwillingly.

This is my dream today, together it will happen,
Come true, move on and make room for the next.

Sarah Chorlton (12)
Newent Community School

I Have A Dream

I have a dream,
Where justice dawns on the darkness of arrogance,
Because every man and woman alive are standing
United on the path of righteousness.

I have a dream,
That the world is not at battle, but is in united world peace.

I have a dream,
Where poverty-stricken children's pleas of hunger
And help are answered.

I have a dream,
That instead of nuclear and atomic bombs
Being hurled at innocent people,
They are carefully helping Third World
Countries to rebuild and remould its cities and houses.
But still this is only a dream,
We can make dreams come true though
Can't we?

Jess Cook (13)
Newent Community School

I Have A Dream

I have a dream that
One day the world will tolerate,
Bigotry will cease.
I have a dream that
Never again a drop of blood
Will be shed over race or religion.
I have a dream that
All people can sit at the round
Table of acceptance.
It is only when we are able to
Accept people's creed and colour
That we can see them for who they are.
I have a dream that
One day our acceptance will
Shine a ray of bright light
On this dark earth.
I have a dream that
One day, my dream is today.

Josh Edwards (13)
Newent Community School

I Have A Dream - Haiku

Our dreams come alive,
Everyone helps each other
And the world is one.

Matthew Gaskins (12)
Newent Community School

I Have A Dream

I have a dream,
>That no one has more than they need,

Or less than they need.
>I have a dream

That food is not scarce,
>In countries where it is needed.

I have a dream,
>That everyone will get along

And there are no wars.
>I have a dream

That no one is persecuted
>For their race and beliefs.

I have a dream,
>That all nations will join together

And stand firm like a rock.
>I have a dream,

Of a wonderful world,
>But it's up to us to change us.

I have a dream.

Ruth Cracknell (12)
Newent Community School

I Have A Dream

I have a dream,
One day the world is a peaceful place,
No guns or bombs killing innocent people,
No words or phrases breaking up friends and family.

I have a dream,
One day world health to everyone,
No babies or children dying before they should,
No hunger in Africa, everyone has the right to food.

I have a dream,
One day everyone will be thought of equally,
No bullies or racists, no killing and hurting people,
No difference between black and white people,
Everyone is the same,

I have a dream,
The world is a peaceful place.

Hannah Lammas (12)
Newent Community School

I Have A Dream

I have a dream where freedom rules,
Where poverty and oppression are barred,
I have a dream of a land where
Nothing is in vain,
I have a dream of a land where a
River of peace flows forever,
This land where there is no sadness
Or pain
And in its place there is hope,
Freedom,
Joy and love.

I have a dream of a world
Where all men are united as one,
Not separated by mere colour or creed,
I have a dream.

Luke Wathen (13)
Newent Community School

I Have A Dream

I have a dream of a world without hatred,
A world without war,
Without terrorism and violence,
A world of peace and harmony,
Where hands join together,
All guns and weapons were destroyed,
That all can join together.

I have a dream of world peace,
That not needed deaths could be avoided,
A world without racism,
Where white and black join together,
I have a dream that poverty is ended,
Where food is shared around,
I have a dream.

Tim Dulson (13)
Newent Community School

I Have A Dream

I have a dream,
When I sleep,
It feels so real,
So strong and deep,
Everyone there is happy and free,
There is enough food to eat for tea,
No one loved gets taken away,
In the streets, no children lay,
Sickness, death and poverty,
Are banished, hurled into the sea,
There is no rubbish spread around,
There are no packets on the ground,
All animals are free to go,
Back to their habitat, desert or snow,
So think of this world and the things
It could do,
Is this the world you dream of too?

Ellie Baggett (11)
Newent Community School

My Dad

He was kind and thoughtful,
He was good to my school,
He was the best dad in the whole world that you have,
When I was ill or down in the dumps,
He was there for me,
He took me to Tesco every week
And he gave me pocket money every weekend,
He spoilt me rotten,
I miss him.

Kelly Marie Andrews (13)
Paternoster Special School

Anne Frank

She was a girl,
She was 12 when she went into hiding,
Why?
Because she was a Jew,
The Nazis want to kill Jews.
She wrote a diary,
It said about her life and feelings.

Aiden Spencer (13)
Paternoster Special School

Kelly Holmes

Kelly's heroes
Are children who want
To run mega
Fast!
They don't want to come
Last
Or they might lose the golden medal
And only have a plastic ribbon.
I like Kelly Holmes.

Cody Davey (13)
Paternoster Special School

I Have A Dream

I have a dream that no one will be left to die
And treat all those poor children who always cry,
To help those in severe poverty or those with no hope,
Great it would be to help people cope,
But better it would be to stop it.

I have a dream to follow good others,
Blanket the world in white, soft covers,
People who don't give up, no matter how they suffer,
Are the ones who deserve to grow even tougher,
But will they be here when the lights are lit?

I have a dream to strip countries of evil,
To get rid of weapons both fatal and lethal,
Never to hear of violence or death,
To take someone's life is cruel and like theft,
But why can't it just stop?

But enough is enough,
Life in this world is tough,
If you're scared to go outside,
You want to run and hide,
You're not the only one.

We're breaking our hearts piece by piece
And I have a dream, to restore global peace,
One day I hope to fulfil this dream,
I bet I'm not the only one, who dreams this same dream.

Shannon Cook (14)
Severn Vale School